The Journey
Study Series
Facilitator's Guide

The Journey Study Series Facilitator's Guide

A Thomas Nelson Study Series
Based on *The Journey*
by
BILLY GRAHAM

THOMAS NELSON
Since 1798

NASHVILLE DALLAS MEXICO CITY RIO DE JANEIRO BEIJING

Additional material written by Terry Hadaway

Published in Nashville, Tennessee. Thomas Nelson is a trademark of Thomas Nelson, Inc.

Thomas Nelson, Inc., titles may be purchased in bulk for educational, business, fund-raising, or sales promotional use. For information, please e-mail SpecialMarkets@ThomasNelson.com.

The Journey *Study Series Facilitator's Guide: A Thomas Nelson Study Series Based on* The Journey *by Billy Graham*

ISBN-13: 978-1-4185-2636-8
ISBN-10: 1-4185-2636-3

Printed in the United States of America

07 08 09 10 11 RRD 5 4 3 2 1

The Journey Study Series

Searching for Hope
Living as a Christian
Leaving a Legacy
Dealing with Doubt
Confronting the Enemies Within
Embracing the Good News
Building a Christ-Centered Home
Learning to Pray
The Facilitator's Guide

CONTENTS

BUILDING A CHRIST-CENTERED HOME

LEARNING TO PRAY

SEARCHING FOR HOPE

CHAPTER ONE

THE UNIVERSAL SEARCH

PREPARE TO LEAD

TO GET THE MOST FROM THIS STUDY, READ THE PREFACE AND pages 3–12 of *The Journey.*

- Read the sidebar on pages 6–7 of the Study Guide, and be prepared to discuss the information in reference to the lesson.
- Read and respond to the entire lesson in the Study Guide. Make note of significant things the Lord teaches you as you study.
- Pray, asking God to reveal to you the truths related to this lesson that are applicable to the class members who will attend the small-group session.

LEADING THE SMALL GROUP

Introduction: Introduce the lesson by highlighting *Think About It* on pages 3–4 in the Study Guide. Write on the board the quote at the beginning of the lesson and the Scripture verse on pages 3–4.

Rewind: Direct participants to identify the number-one goals of most people they know. Quickly summarize the opinions of the class, listing the top three responses on the board. Ask participants to respond to the second question in the activity, in which they are asked to identify what their behavior reveals about their goals in life. Draw a horizontal line stretching across the board. At the far left, place an X representing life's beginning. At the far right, place an X representing life's end. Ask: *What do you plan to do with the space between these two bookends?* Call for responses.

Direct participants to take a few moments to respond to the question regarding their eternal destinations. Ask anyone who has questions regarding this activity to see you after class or to speak with a church staff member. Call for volunteers to read aloud the following passages. Discuss the meaning of each passage. The correct answers to the activity are shown below:

a. Matthew 7:21—Not everyone who calls Jesus "Lord" will enter heaven.

b. James 2:19—Believing God exists isn't enough.

c. Matthew 19:16–24—Keeping God's commandments doesn't guarantee entrance to heaven.

Ask a volunteer to read aloud selected verses from Psalm 139:1–24. Ask participants to write a brief description of their purpose in life. Be prepared to discuss possible responses.

Rethink: Call attention to the activity in which participants are asked to mark the words that describe their life journeys. Call for volunteers to share some of their responses. Point out that life is full of twists and turns that complicate life and make it unpredictable. Direct participants to mark the concerns with which they are currently dealing. Ask: *Do you want your life to be better or worse in the future?* Call for responses. Point out that life will change only as we change and allow God to take more control of our lives.

Reflect: Be prepared to list on the board the main points of this lesson. Rely on the information in the Study Guide and in the book to support your discussion.

1. **God put you on this journey.** Ask a volunteer to read aloud Jeremiah 29:11. Ask: *What is the difference between God having a plan for people and people having a plan for God? Which one is your life philosophy?*

2. **God wants to join you on the journey.** Ask volunteers to read aloud Deuteronomy 31:8 and Matthew 28:20. Ask: *What does each of these passages say about God's desire to be close to His people?* Read aloud 1 Corinthians 1:9. Ask: *What is the universal calling of all people?*

3. **God calls you to a new journey.** Ask participants to reflect on their lives one, five, and twenty years from now. Ask them to also consider their futures in eternity. Direct participants to evaluate their certainty about world peace, job security, vocation, weather, and eternity.

React: What will be the lasting impact of this lesson? There are some truths that must be considered:

1. *The old path will never deliver what it promises.* What is the difference between your old path and your new path? Read aloud Luke 12:19–20 and point out the mistakes in judgment made by the man.

2. *God's path always delivers what He promises.* What does God promise? How certain are you that God will deliver on His promises? Read aloud Philippians 4:7. Why don't we experience peace the way God describes it?

3. *God's path will lead you home.* There are only two paths in life—the path to heaven and the path to hell. Because God loves us, He gives us the opportunity to choose the path we want to travel. It is a choice we all must make personally; no one can make it for us. Read Hebrews 11:13–16. Ask participants to carefully consider how they have responded to God's invitation to eternal life.

Call attention to the "Three Truths" activity at the end of the lesson. Be prepared to share your three truths as an example. Close in prayer.

SEARCHING FOR HOPE

CHAPTER 2

THE SEARCH FOR GOD

PREPARE TO LEAD

TO GET THE MOST FROM THIS STUDY, READ PAGES 13–18 OF *The Journey.*

- Read the sidebar on pages 23–24 of the Study Guide and be prepared to discuss the information in reference to the lesson.

- Read and respond to the entire lesson in the Study Guide. Make note of significant things the Lord teaches you as you study.

- Pray, asking God to reveal to you the truths related to this lesson that are applicable to the class members who will attend the small-group session.

LEADING THE SMALL GROUP

Introduction: Introduce the lesson by highlighting *Think About It* on pages 19–20 in the Study Guide. Write on the board the quote at the beginning of the lesson and the Scripture verse on pages 19–20.

Rewind: Direct participants to identify the images of God that have been a part of their perceptions. Ask volunteers to explain why they had certain images. Compare those images to the scriptural images, and ask volunteers to explain any differences.

Call attention to the matching activity. Call on volunteers to read each Scripture passage. The correct responses are as follows:

a. Acts 14:17—God has given us rain and crops.

b. Romans 1:20—Creation gives evidence of God's existence.

c. Psalm 100:25—The stars and the sky are evidence of God's existence.

Ask participants to identify some things they believe that cannot be proven true. List responses on the board. Ask them to identify the reasons they believe these things to be true. Be prepared to discuss the sidebar related to Psalm 115.

Rethink: Ask participants to identify evidences of God's existence that they see in everyday life. List responses on the board. Direct participants to identify some things people do to try to maintain or establish a relationship with God. Be prepared to discuss the value of each activity in response to an authentic relationship with God. Point out that the activities cannot take the place of a real relationship with Him. Discuss the importance of communicating with God, and ask participants to identify the regularity and occasions in which they communicate with Him. Ask: *If you communicated with your closest relative, spouse, or friend as often as you communicate with God, what kind of relationship would you have?*

Reflect: Be prepared to list on the board the main points of this lesson. Rely on the information in the Study Guide and in the book to support your discussion.

1. **God has spoken to us through a book: the Bible.** Invite a volunteer to read aloud Hebrews 1:1. Ask: *How has God spoken to us?* Read aloud 2 Peter 1:20–21. Ask: *What inspired the prophets to speak?* God wants to communicate with us in ways that we understand. By having His written Word, we can eliminate confusion as to what He really said.

2. **God has spoken to us through a Person: Jesus Christ.** Jesus came as a physical revelation of God to man. Read Colossians 2:9 and John 1:14. Ask: *What do these verses say about Jesus' identity?*

Anyone who wants to doubt God's revelation will not be convinced through the Bible or discussions about Jesus. What doubters need to see is the reality of God's being alive in the lives of real people. A doubting world can't deny what they see happen in the lives of people they know.

React: Ask: *What is the difference between knowing someone and knowing about someone? Do you believe our culture is a Christian culture? Why or why not?*

Direct participants to work through the activity at the end of the lesson in which they are asked to describe their faith relationship with God. Be prepared to share your own story by completing the following tasks:

1. Describe your life before you had a relationship with God.
2. What was it that made you realize your need for God?
3. Describe when and how you asked for forgiveness and invited Jesus Christ into your life.
4. How has your life been different since that time? What difference does God make in your daily life?

The activity above will lead participants to develop a contemporary version of their testimonies. It is important to be prepared to share our testimonies with anyone at any time. If time permits, allow time for participants to pair up and practice sharing their testimonies. Be prepared to help anyone who is having a difficult time with this activity.

Call attention to the "Three Truths" activity at the end of the lesson. Be prepared to share your three truths as an example. Close in prayer.

SEARCHING FOR HOPE

CHAPTER 3

WHAT IS GOD LIKE?

PREPARE TO LEAD

TO GET THE MOST FROM THIS STUDY GUIDE, READ PAGES 18–22 of *The Journey.*

- Read the sidebar on pages 42–44 of the Study Guide, and be prepared to discuss the information in reference to the lesson.

- Read and respond to the entire lesson in the Study Guide. Make note of significant things the Lord teaches you as you study.

- Pray, asking God to reveal to you the truths related to this lesson that are applicable to the class members who will attend the small-group session.

LEADING THE SMALL GROUP

Introduction: Introduce the lesson by highlighting *Think About It* on pages 37–38 in the Study Guide. Write on the board the quote at the beginning of the lesson and the Scripture verse on pages 37–38.

Rewind: Direct participants to identify sources for the images of God that have been a part of their perceptions. Write on the board: **God is like . . .** Call for volunteers to complete the statement. Discuss some of the ways God has been presented in movies, in books, and on television. Point out that any attempt to define God places limits on Him and, therefore, is inadequate. Ask participants to identify common misconceptions about God. List responses on the board.

Call for volunteers to read aloud each of the following Scripture passages. Discuss what each one says about God.

Psalm 102:27

Malachi 3:6

Hebrews 1:12

James 1:17

Write on the board: **Four Truths about God.** As the discussion progresses, list each truth and related Scripture under the heading. Begin by asking participants what comes to mind when they hear the word *spirit.* Ask: *How does your concept of spirit affect your concept of God?* Discuss responses.

Write the first truth on the board—**God Is a Spirit.** Based on Jesus' words in John 4:24 and Luke 24:39, what was Jesus' concept of God? As you discuss God as Spirit, be prepared to relate the information in the sidebar regarding God's leadership of His people through His Spirit.

Write the second truth on the board—**God Is a Person.** Ask participants to identify the characteristics of humans that are most like God. Ask: *Why are our traits different from God's traits?* Discuss responses, pointing out that our traits are affected by sin; God possesses these traits in their perfect form.

Write the third truth on the board—**God Is Holy.** Ask participants to suggest meanings for the word *holy. Holy* means set apart for a purpose. Ask participants to list some things that society accepts but God condemns. Discuss the changes in the social attitude and the potential reasons for the changes. What do the following Scriptures say about God's character? Habakkuk 1:13; Isaiah 6:3; 1 John 1:5; and Revelation 4:8.

Write the fourth truth on the board—**God Is Love.** Direct participants to identify how love affects their lives. Discuss responses. Ask: *What does your experience with love reveal about God's character?*

Rethink: Ask a volunteer to read aloud Jeremiah 31:3 and ask participants to discuss reactions to the verse. Ask: *What are some things in which we place our hope?* List responses on the board. Ask: *What is God doing in your life right now? What has happened to move you closer to God?* Call for responses. Ask: *What has happened that moved you away from God?* Call for responses.

Reflect: Be prepared to list on the board the main points of this lesson. Rely on the information in the Study Guide and in the book to support your discussion.

Ask: *Why do people place their hope in anything other than God? What keeps you from living with the realization of the hope of God?* Discuss responses. Point out the futility of living with hope in anything other than God.

React: Ask: *What are the possible responses to the truth about God?* There are only two possible responses:

1. **Walk away because your hope is in something else.** Read Matthew 19:16–22 and identify the man's misplaced hope.
2. **Place your hope in Jesus Christ and live in obedience to Him.** Read Acts 8:26–40 and compare the response of the Ethiopian to the man in the Matthew passage.

Ask: *Which response best characterizes your life?* If you perceive your class to be less mature believers, you might consider taking time to share a little about what it means to accept Jesus Christ as Lord and Savior. If the class is more mature in its faith, consider discussing what it means to live in obedience to God. Challenge the class to make their faith the guiding force in their lives.

Call attention to the "Three Truths" activity at the end of the lesson. Be prepared to share your three truths as an example. Close in prayer.

SEARCHING FOR HOPE

CHAPTER FOUR

WHO AM I?

PREPARE TO LEAD

TO GET THE MOST FROM THIS STUDY GUIDE, READ PAGES 23–27 of *The Journey.*

- Read the sidebar on pages 61–62 of the Study Guide, and be prepared to discuss the information in reference to the lesson.
- Read and respond to the entire lesson in the Study Guide. Make note of significant things the Lord teaches you as you study.
- Pray, asking God to reveal to you the truths related to this lesson that are applicable to the class members who will attend the small-group session.

LEADING THE SMALL GROUP

Introduction: Introduce the lesson by highlighting *Think About It* on pages 57–58 in the Study Guide. Write on the board the quote at the beginning of the lesson and the Scripture verse on page 57.

Rewind: Discuss the qualities of a good relationship, then ask participants to characterize their relationships with God using the activity in the Study Guide. Discuss the ways that Christians are perceived by family and friends. Identify some reasons people don't see us the same way we see ourselves. Point out that sometimes we see ourselves the way we want to be seen rather than the way we really are. The tension between reality and the ideal leads us to have restless hearts. It is these restless hearts that motivate us to seek solutions to our problems.

Ask: *What does it mean to have a restless heart? What does your restless heart cause you to do?* Discuss responses. Point out that the inner restlessness often has spiritual implications. Call for volunteers to talk about times when God has used their restlessness to guide them. Ask: *What interferes with your relationship with God?* List responses on the board.

Rethink: Point out that Scripture says we are created in God's image. Ask: *What does it mean to be created in God's image? What value does that assign to us?* Allow participants to discuss their responses in small groups. Discuss how being created in the image of God can get out of control. Why do some people see themselves as invincible and beyond being accountable to God?

Make two columns on the board. Label one **Adam and Eve** and the other one **Us**. Begin by writing in both columns "created to be God's friends forever." Call for a volunteer to read aloud Matthew 16:26. Ask participants to identify the two priorities Jesus pointed out. Ask: *Of the two priorities, which is more important to people today?*

Read Psalm 8:5. Ask: *Because people are made a little lower than heavenly beings, what should be our attitudes toward each other? How do God's ways of doing things compare to our ways? When we mistreat people, what does it say about our understanding of this Scripture?* Allow time for participants to discuss the ways in which we devalue each other.

Discuss the concept of friendship. Ask: *What criteria do we use when selecting friends?* Refer to the activity in the Study Guide in response to this question. Ask: *Why would God want to be friends with us?* List responses on the board.

Reflect: Ask: *What are some things that promise happiness and fulfillment but fail to deliver?* List responses on the board. Ask: *What are some things you have tried in order to achieve happiness and fulfillment?* Refer to the activity in the Study Guide. Ask: *What do people do when they realize their efforts to achieve happiness and fulfillment have come up short?*

React: Read aloud Proverbs 18:24. Ask: *How does being friends with God affect your daily life? What interferes with your ability to see yourself as God's friend?* Read aloud John 15:15. Ask: *What is Jesus' attitude toward those who trust Him as Savior and Lord?*

When you get to the end of this study, you will have challenged people regarding their relationships with God. It is possible that some people have yet to settle that issue and, therefore, will be uncomfortable discussing this issue. Be sensitive to these people and make it a point to speak with them after the class regarding their relationship with God. As always, be prepared to share your thoughts and your experience.

Call attention to the "Three Truths" activity at the end of the lesson. Be prepared to share your three truths as an example. Close in prayer.

SEARCHING FOR HOPE

CHAPTER FIVE

STARTING OVER

PREPARE TO LEAD

TO GET THE MOST FROM THIS STUDY GUIDE, READ PAGES 43–52 of *The Journey.*

- Read the sidebar on pages 77–78 of the Study Guide, and be prepared to discuss the information in reference to the lesson.

- Read and respond to the entire lesson in the Study Guide. Make note of significant things the Lord teaches you as you study.

- Pray, asking God to reveal to you the truths related to this lesson that are applicable to the class members who will attend the small-group session.

LEADING THE SMALL GROUP

Introduction: Introduce the lesson by highlighting *Think About It* on pages 73–74 in the Study Guide. Write on the board the quote at the beginning of the lesson and the Scripture verse on page 73.

Rewind: Ask participants to identify some of the things they have tried in an effort to solve problems in life. Discuss the outcome of their efforts to solve problems. Write on the board **Our Greatest Need** and call for volunteers to suggest what they think is our greatest need and the things people do to try to meet that need. List responses on the board.

Point out that going in a new direction requires the admission of the fact that we are going in the wrong direction. Ask: *Why is it so difficult to admit we are headed in the wrong direction?* Enlist a volunteer to read aloud Matthew 7:13. Discuss this verse and what it says about the need to change paths in life. Call for a volunteer to read Jeremiah 6:16. Ask participants to discuss this verse in response to the need to change paths.

Draw a horizontal line on the board. Then draw a vertical line that intersects the horizontal line in the middle. At the right end of the horizontal line, write **Death and Destruction**. At the top of the vertical line, write **Eternal Peace**. Trace the horizontal line, referring to it as being the natural path of life. Point out that everyone comes to this intersection, where they must willfully change courses. We refer to this willful change of directions as salvation.

Call attention to the sidebar on pages 77–78 and discuss the concept of sin. Ask participants to suggest what today's culture considers to be sin and how that concept relates to the biblical ideal. If your class is primarily mature believers, a thorough study of the sidebar might be more applicable.

Call for a volunteer to read aloud James 2:10. Ask: *Is living the sinless life possible? Why or why not?* Read John 14:6 and discuss God's solution to our problem. Refer to the line drawing on the board and point out that eternal peace is both present and future. Also point out that eternal peace is only associated with one of the lines. The natural life cannot lead to eternal peace, no matter what we do.

Rethink: Ask participants to use the Study Guide activity to identify who they believe Jesus was. Reread John 14:6. Then read John 1:1 and John 1:14. Ask: *How do these verses answer that question?* Arrange the class in three small groups (if possible) and assign one of the following Scripture verses to each group, asking them to read the verse and to summarize what each says about Jesus: John 10:30; John 14:9; and Matthew 17:5. Call for the individual groups (or individuals) to report their findings. Discuss the significance of each verse. It is not enough to know who Jesus is; we also must know what He did.

Reflect: Jesus did four things that changed the way we relate to God.

1. **Jesus was the sacrifice for sin.** The Old Testament system required a blood sacrifice to atone for sin. There were regulations regarding acceptable sacrifices. Jesus was the ultimate in acceptable sacrifices, and He eliminated the need for continued animal sacrifices. Read aloud Hebrews 9:26 and discuss how Jesus' sacrifice differed from the traditional sacrifices.

2. **Jesus was our substitute.** Read Genesis 22:1–19 and discuss how difficult it would be to do what Abraham did. God followed through in offering His Son as a sacrifice so that you and I will not be held responsible for our sin. Read 2 Corinthians 5:21. Ask: *How does this reality affect your life?*

3. **Jesus was our redeemer.** Call for volunteers to read aloud Matthew 20:28 and 1 Timothy 2:5–6. Use the activity in the Study Guide to discuss who paid the ransom so that we can be freed from sin's captivity.

4. **Jesus was our conqueror.** Jesus won the battle we couldn't win and transferred the victory to each of us. Because Jesus won, we won. Read aloud Colossians 2:15. Ask: *Over what was Jesus victorious?*

React: There are three steps in the salvation process. Refer to the Study Guide for each of the steps and challenge participants to mark the appropriate column in response to each step. Use your personal testimony to point out that you have completed each step.

If you have people who might need to make a decision for Christ, the remaining information in the Study Guide will be valuable to you. Briefly review the steps and call attention to the fact that these steps will be helpful in dealing with unbelievers.

Call attention to the "Three Truths" activity at the end of the lesson. Be prepared to share your three truths as an example. Close in prayer.

SEARCHING FOR HOPE

CHAPTER SIX

A NEW BEGINNING

PREPARE TO LEAD

TO GET THE MOST FROM THIS STUDY GUIDE, READ PAGES 53–62 of *The Journey.*

- Read the sidebar on pages 98–99 of the Study Guide, and be prepared to discuss the information in reference to the lesson.
- Read and respond to the entire lesson in the Study Guide. Make note of significant things the Lord teaches you as you study.
- Pray, asking God to reveal to you the truths related to this lesson that are applicable to the class members who will attend the small-group session.

LEADING THE SMALL GROUP

Introduction: Introduce the lesson by highlighting *Think About It* on pages 93–94 in the Study Guide. Write on the board the quote at the beginning of the lesson and the Scripture verse on page 93.

Rewind: Refer to the activity in the Study Guide and ask participants to mark the statement that best describes their spiritual journeys. Call for a show of hands as you read the possible responses. Point out that we all come to Jesus in different ways and different times, but the one common thread is that we see the need to accept His offer of eternal life. Ask volunteers to suggest their biggest decisions in life. Ask: *On the list of "most important decisions," where is "accepted Jesus Christ as my Lord"?*

What we have been is not nearly as important as what we are becoming. Tell the story of Paul's conversion and the fact that he had been the worst of the worst before being remade into a powerful missionary. Ask participants to consider what God is doing in their lives. Call for volunteers to report some of the things that are happening in their lives. Read 2 Corinthians 6:2. Ask: *When is the right time to give one's life to Christ? Why is this true?*

Draw a time line on the board and ask participants to consider their present spiritual conditions as compared to their past spiritual lives. Ask: *Are you growing closer to God and more excited about your faith or farther from God and less excited about your faith? What are the causes of both possibilities?* Read 2 Corinthians 5:17 and discuss its meaning.

Rethink: What happens when God makes all things new? The following seven things are the primary points in this lesson.

1. **A New Relationship.** Ephesians 2:12 reveals the "before" picture, while Romans 5:1 shows the "after" picture. Enlist a volunteer to read each verse, and ask participants to suggest brief contemporary summaries for each verse. Direct participants to record their thoughts in the space provided in the Study Guide. Discuss the benefits of being God's friend. List responses on the board. The following are the correct responses to the matching activity in the Study Guide. Read aloud each passage, and discuss the correct responses.

   1 Peter 1:23—You are born again through God's Word.

   Ephesians 1:5—You are adopted into God's family.

   John 3:4—You must be born again.

   Ephesians 5:1—You must imitate God.

2. **A New Citizenship.** Discuss the privileges and responsibilities associated with being a citizen of a country. Ask: *What are the privileges and responsibilities associated with being a citizen of the kingdom of God?* Invite a volunteer to read aloud Philippians 3:20 and Acts 5:29. Discuss the appropriate biblical response when human laws and God's laws contradict each other.

3. **A New Family.** Relate the physical family to the spiritual family of God—the church. Instruct participants to rate their commitment to their church. Ask why people would associate with the church but not be committed to it. Discuss responses. Call for the class to suggest some things that can help improve one's commitment to the church.

4. **A New Purpose.** Call attention to Ephesians 2:10. Ask: *Why does God leave us here after we accept Jesus as Lord and Savior?* Use the activity in the Study Guide to discuss this question.

5. **A New Power.** Read Romans 8:9. Use the Study Guide to discuss the possible proofs that we belong to God. Point out that emotions, though part of the spiritual life, aren't a reliable proof of one's relationship with God.

Reflect: The sixth thing that happens when we become believers is more future-centered than present-centered.

6. **A New Destiny.** Discuss the change in destination—from hell to heaven—and how that should affect the daily lives of people who know Jesus Christ. Ask a volunteer to read aloud Romans 6:23. Ask: *What can we do to earn eternal life?* (Nothing.) Read 1 Peter 1:3–4 and discuss the durability of our salvation.

React: What is the final thing that happens when we give our lives to Jesus Christ?

7. **A New Journey.** Ask: *What is the difference between* becoming *a Christian and* being *a Christian?* Be prepared to share a personal story about your journey and about what God is doing in your life to grow and mature your faith.

Call attention to the "Three Truths" activity at the end of the lesson. Be prepared to share your three truths as an example. Close in prayer.

LIVING AS A CHRISTIAN

CHAPTER ONE

STARTING STRONG

PREPARE TO LEAD

TO GET THE MOST FROM THIS STUDY, READ THE PREFACE AND pages 74–77 of *The Journey.*

- Read the sidebar on pages 6–7 of the Study Guide, and be prepared to discuss the information in reference to the lesson.

- Read and respond to the entire lesson in the Study Guide. Make note of significant things the Lord teaches you as you study.

- Pray, asking God to reveal to you the truths related to this lesson that are applicable to the class members who will attend the small-group session.

LEADING THE SMALL GROUP

Introduction: Introduce the lesson by highlighting *Think About It* on pages 3–4 in the Study Guide. Write on the board the quote at the beginning of the lesson and the Scripture verse on page 3.

Rewind: Discuss reasons people don't grow spiritually. List responses on the board. Ask participants to identify some of the things that negatively affect their spiritual growth. Discuss the possible consequences of not growing spiritually. Call for volunteers to read Hebrews 6:1 and 1 Peter 2:2. Identify the common theme in these verses. Discuss situations in which spiritual immaturity has hampered your effectiveness for God. Point back to examples from the lives of the Israelites and other biblical personalities. Call attention to the fact that all people battle spiritual immaturity and its effects in their lives.

Read the sidebar about what it means to be a carnal Christian, and relate the information to the concept of spiritual immaturity. Read 1 Peter 2:11 and talk about the various sources of fleshly lusts.

Rethink: Direct participants to the activity in the Study Guide in which they are asked to evaluate their time commitments to specific activities. Once the class has had time to complete the activity, call for someone to record the total hours from each person present and to average those numbers to reveal an average number of hours that are "promised" during the day. Don't be surprised if the total is greater than twenty-four hours. Ask volunteers to suggest things they do that are not on the list. Point out that "spending time with God" also doesn't appear on the list. Carefully evaluate the number of hours spent in spiritual growth each week. Ask how many of those hours are spent at church and how much in personal time. Call for participants to evaluate where they are in their spiritual lives and the direction they are headed. Discuss the importance of investing time in things that lead to spiritual growth. Be prepared to make the class aware of the spiritual growth opportunities that are offered through your church.

Reflect: Evaluate the spiritual maturity of people in the class using the following criteria (also listed in the Study Guide). Briefly highlight the relationship between Paul and the Thessalonians. Call for a volunteer to read 2 Thessalonians 1:3–12.

1. **Is your love for other believers growing?** (2 Thessalonians 1:3). Ask participants to suggest things for which they are willing to be inconvenienced. List responses on the board. Ask: *For what are you willing to make sacrifices?* Reread 2 Thessalonians 1:3. Ask: *Could Paul's words to the Thessalonians be said about you? Why or why not?*

2. **Is your faith a topic of conversation among other believers?** (2 Thessalonians 1:4–5). Ask: *When people talk about you, what qualities are they discussing? Why don't people talk about your faith?* Point to the activity in the Study Guide in which participants are asked to identify what happens when life falls apart. Discuss the possible consequences related to each choice. Ask: *How might your responses to difficult situations affect the faith or potential faith of other people?*

3. **Is God's work your work?** (2 Thessalonians 1:11–12). Ask: *Are you attempting to bring God into what you do, or are you trying to move into the work God is doing? What is the difference in these two approaches?*

React: Read aloud 1 Corinthians 3:1. Ask: *What is the difference between being spiritual and being worldly? When you consider the influences in your life, do you have more influences pushing you toward being spiritual or worldly? If you have more spiritual influences, what is the tone of your life likely to be? If you have more worldly influences, what is the tone of your life likely to be?*

Point out the four steps to spiritual maturity in the Study Guide. Write each step on the board as you discuss it.

1. *Commit to spending time with God daily.*
2. *Focus on allowing God to work through you to meet the needs of someone else.*
3. *Spend time reflecting on your day from God's perspective.*
4. *Keep a spiritual journal.*

Be willing to share your personal spiritual routine, and encourage others to consider developing a similar routine.

Call attention to the "Three Truths" activity at the end of the lesson. Be prepared to share your three truths as an example. Close in prayer.

LIVING AS A CHRISTIAN

CHAPTER TWO

OBSTACLES ALONG THE WAY

PREPARE TO LEAD

TO GET THE MOST FROM THIS STUDY, READ PAGES 77–82 OF *The Journey.*

- Read the sidebar on pages 24–25 of the Study Guide, and be prepared to discuss the information in reference to the lesson.
- Read and respond to the entire lesson in the Study Guide. Make note of significant things the Lord teaches you as you study.
- Pray, asking God to reveal to you the truths related to this lesson that are applicable to the class members who will attend the small-group session.

LEADING THE SMALL GROUP

Introduction: Introduce the lesson by highlighting *Think About It* on pages 21–22 in the Study Guide. Write on the board the quote at the beginning of the lesson and the Scripture verse on page 21.

Rewind: Discuss the two aspects of salvation—present and future. Call attention to the activity in the Study Guide, and ask participants to determine which activity is their primary focus. Ask: *What are some things that interfere with your ability or desire to grow spiritually?* List responses on the board. Ask: *What are some of the spiritual obstacles that we all face? What happens when we encounter these obstacles? Why are these obstacles present in our lives?* Read aloud John 10:10. Ask: *What are the two conditions in this verse?* (destruction versus abundant life). *What causes people to change their commitment to spiritual growth?* List responses on the board. Ask: *Have any of these things happened to you?*

Use the sidebar to discuss the biblical concept of being a disciple. Point out that in the first century, people had the option of selecting their teachers. As disciples, they were responsible not only for knowing their teacher's tenets, but also for living them out. In today's church, many people want to stop at knowing what to believe without getting to the point of actually living it.

Rethink: Direct participants to use the activity in the Study Guide to evaluate the difficulty of routine chores. Ask them then to determine if anything on the list might be an obstacle to their spiritual growth. Read aloud 2 Peter 3:18 then direct participants to evaluate Peter's words using the activity in the Study Guide. Call for a volunteer to read aloud Romans 8:29, then ask a volunteer to identify the image to which we are commanded to conform.

Point out that it is God's will that we be conformed to His image. In a later lesson, we will get into the concept of God's will and what it means to each person.

Reflect: Discuss the key to spiritual maturity and how believers approach the concept of spiritual maturity. Call for volunteers to identify the daily struggles they face and to suggest how those struggles affect their spiritual lives. Write the following two statements on the board, and ask participants to identify the statement that best represents their lives:

I am a positive spiritual influence on the world.

I am letting the world influence my spiritual life.

Point out that one of these two statements is true about every person.

How can we become a positive influence on the world around us?

1. **Daily submit every area of life to His authority.** Read aloud Luke 9:23. Ask: *What does it mean to deny yourself daily? How do you do that? What areas of life are most difficult to turn over to God? Why is it so hard to turn these areas over to God?*

Reread Luke 9:23. Ask: *What are the three actions required to follow Christ?* Call attention to the Study Guide activity that asks participants to rate God's control over specific areas of life. Encourage participants to spend time working on their greatest weaknesses.

2. **Involve God in the battle for your will.** Read aloud John 3:30 and ask participants to honestly identify their main focus in life. If you do not plan to grow spiritually, you will not grow! Ask: *Is Satan more concerned about your decisions or your commitments? Why?* Many Christians live in spiritual lethargy because they are afraid to give God the attention they should. Instead, they give their attention to things that don't really matter.

3. **Embrace the new life.** Read aloud John 15:11 and discuss the freedom that accompanies being a child of God. Jesus had no problem keeping things in proper perspective. Use the activity in the Study Guide to compare Jesus' focus on certain aspects of life to our commitment to those aspects of life.

React: Use the section in the Study Guide to lead the discussion of the meaning of this lesson in the daily lives of believers. Read aloud Romans 12:2 and identify what God wants to renew in each of us. Ask: *What is the end result of this change?* (Ideally it will be an awareness of and commitment to doing God's will.) Allow time for participants to rewrite Romans 12:2 as a prayer for their lives. Call for a few volunteers to share their prayers.

Call attention to the "Three Truths" activity at the end of the lesson. Be prepared to share your three truths as an example. Close in prayer.

LIVING AS A CHRISTIAN

CHAPTER THREE

IT'S A MARATHON

PREPARE TO LEAD

TO GET THE MOST FROM THIS STUDY, READ PAGES 85–89 OF *The Journey.*

- Read the sidebar on pages 42–43 of the Study Guide, and be prepared to discuss the information in reference to the lesson.
- Read and respond to the entire lesson in the Study Guide. Make note of significant things the Lord teaches you as you study.
- Pray, asking God to reveal to you the truths related to this lesson that are applicable to the class members who will attend the small-group session.

LEADING THE SMALL GROUP

Introduction: Introduce the lesson by highlighting *Think About It* on pages 39–40 in the Study Guide. Write on the board the quote at the beginning of the lesson and the Scripture verse on page 39.

Rewind: Ask participants to suggest some things for which a person might train. List responses on the board. Call for volunteers to identify specific training they have had and the task for which the training was necessary. Be prepared to speak about specific training you have received and how it has benefited you. Transition into the discussion about spiritual training by calling attention to the activity under the Rewind heading. Discuss the differing degrees of spiritual preparation and how people in each category might present themselves in your church.

Write **Endurance** on the board, and ask volunteers to suggest meanings or synonyms for the word. List responses on the board. Call for a volunteer to read aloud Hebrews 12:1–2 and discuss the biblical picture of endurance. Call for volunteers to discuss some things they have had to endure and the spiritual growth that their endurance produced. Briefly discuss some of the things people can do to build their spiritual strength.

If time allows, use the sidebar to discuss the concept of "witness." Point out that witness should be a lifestyle for all believers, not an activity for the spiritually elite.

Rethink: Because people are multitasking, there seems to be a sense of urgency about many activities that we might prefer to take more slowly. Ask: *What are* *some things that we hurry through?* List responses on the board. Direct participants to use the activity in the Study Guide to identify how their hurrying affects their attention to detail. Call for a volunteer to read aloud Hebrews 5:12–14. After reviewing the passage, determine the problem being addressed by the author. The problem in the church was the lack of spiritual growth. Discuss how we often get "going to church" and "growing spiritually" confused. Ask participants which one is more important. Point out that we often make a bigger deal out of going to church than growing spiritually.

Reflect: Be prepared to discuss a struggle you have faced that has produced spiritual growth in your life. Call for a few volunteers to briefly share similar experiences. Point out that struggles in life are common and should be viewed as God's way to produce spiritual growth in our lives. Ask: *Why don't people grow spiritually through their struggles?* Discuss responses.

Call for a volunteer to read aloud Philippians 1:27–30. Use the following outline to guide your discussion of this biblical pattern for dealing with life's difficulties:

1. **Let your commitment to Christ guide your conduct** (1:27a). Arrange the class in small groups, and ask them to identify the responsibilities associated with being a Christian and with being a citizen. After a few minutes, call for groups to report. List common answers on the board. Ask participants how they deal with the tension between these two responsibilities. Discuss responses.

2. **Seek the support of other believers** (1:27b). Be prepared to highlight the opportunities provided by your church for fellowship and

socializing. Point out that the social aspect of the faith is necessary if we are going to be in a position to help each other in times of need. Use the activity in the Study Guide to identify things that prevent believers from establishing and maintaining relationships with other believers. Discuss how to prevent these things from happening, focusing on developing an atmosphere of trust.

3. Focus on God, not on your problems (1:28–30). Ask: *Why does Satan want believers focused on their problems?* Discuss responses. Lead the class to discover the adversaries that attack them. List responses in the spaces provided in the Study Guide. Discuss some things that can be done so that believers will remember God's promises even in the midst of their struggles.

Point out that problems are a part of life; it is the Christian's response to problems that distinguishes him or her from non-believers. Ask participants to consider what their responses to problems say about God and their relationships with Him.

React: As time allows, call for volunteers to read aloud Philippians 4:13; 2 Chronicles 15:7; Isaiah 35:4; 1 Corinthians 16:13; and Ephesians 6:10–13. Discuss the message regarding spiritual growth presented in each passage. Point out that God's message is consistent across the testaments and across generations.

Call attention to the "Three Truths" activity at the end of the lesson. Be prepared to share your three truths as an example. Close in prayer.

LIVING AS A CHRISTIAN

CHAPTER FOUR

THE CALL TO DISCIPLESHIP

PREPARE TO LEAD

TO GET THE MOST FROM THIS STUDY, READ PAGES 89–93 OF *The Journey.*

- Read the sidebar on pages 58–60 of the Study Guide, and be prepared to discuss the information in reference to the lesson.
- Read and respond to the entire lesson in the Study Guide. Make note of significant things the Lord teaches you as you study.
- Pray, asking God to reveal to you the truths related to this lesson that are applicable to the class members who will attend the small-group session.

LEADING THE SMALL GROUP

Introduction: Introduce the lesson by highlighting *Think About It* on pages 55–56 in the Study Guide. Write on the board the quote at the beginning of the lesson and the Scripture verse on pages 55–56.

Rewind: On the board, reproduce the spiritual growth chart from page 57 of the lesson in the Study Guide. Be prepared to plot your spiritual growth over the past twelve months and identify the events that were associated with the peaks and valleys in your chart. Encourage participants to chart their spiritual growth over the past year and to identify the causes for their peaks and valleys.

The Study Guide contains a brief description of the way the discipleship model was developed and used to extend a philosophy or school of thought. Ask: *Who are those over whom you exercise some degree of authority or influence? Who has influence over you?* Discuss responses. Point out that we all are disciples and disciplers.

If time allows, use the sidebar on education to highlight some of the biblical patterns of education and how those patterns can be used to strengthen the spiritual walk of every believer today.

Rethink: Call for participants to reflect on some of their most valuable spiritual education experiences and most influential spiritual teachers. Discuss the qualities that make someone a valuable teacher or an experience a valuable experience. List responses on the board. Ask: *When it comes to education, what do you expect of yourself or of your children—As, Bs, Cs, Ds, Fs?* Use the question to transition into a time of reflection regarding spiritual growth. Direct participants to use the Study Guide to evaluate their spiritual growth using the academic scale.

Reflect: Write on the board **Disciple** and **Follower**. Ask participants to describe the differences between these two words in relation to one's spiritual life. Point out the following facts about a disciple.

1. **A disciple is a learner or a student.** Disciples put themselves in positions to learn from their teachers. Discipleship necessitates a personal relationship and confidence in each other. Allow time for participants to work in small groups or in pairs to identify the characteristics of a close personal relationship. After a few moments, call for each group or pair to present its findings. List responses on the board. Ask: *How would you rate your personal relationship with your family, spouse, co-workers, and neighbors?* Use a scale of 1 to 5. Ask: *How would you rate your relationship with Jesus?*

Call for volunteers to read aloud the following Scripture passages. Identify the common theme in the passages.

Psalm 119:45

Isaiah 61:1

Romans 8:20–21

2 Corinthians 3:17

James 1:25

The common theme in the passages above is liberty or freedom. Discuss the dangers of Christian liberty. Ask: *How can Christian liberty be misused?* Read Galatians 5:13 and point out that God's definition of right and wrong limits Christian freedom.

2. **A disciple is a follower.** Read aloud John 13:35. Ask: *What is it that identifies a true follower of Jesus Christ?* Point out that true followers are identified by their love. Guide participants to use the activities in the Study Guide to evaluate their love and its reflection on their relationships with God. Read aloud James 2:14–26 and discuss the relationship between faith and works, pointing out that faith precedes works. In other words, you can't do enough to earn salvation.

3. **A disciple is a servant.** Read aloud Matthew 20:20–24. Write on the board the following two statements:

   I am being served.

   I am serving others.

Ask participants to reflect on the two statements and to determine which one best represents their lives. Read Matthew 20:25–28 and discuss which role is best fitted to someone claiming to be a follower of Jesus Christ.

React: Use the React section of the Study Guide to lead participants to discover how this lesson applies to their daily lives and to discover some things they can do to strengthen their relationship with Christ. Pay particular attention to the concept of servanthood and the service opportunities that are available through your church.

Call attention to the "Three Truths" activity at the end of the lesson. Be prepared to share your three truths as an example. Close in prayer.

LIVING AS A CHRISTIAN

CHAPTER FIVE

OUR UNFAILING GUIDE

PREPARE TO LEAD

TO GET THE MOST FROM THIS STUDY, READ PAGES 104–113 OF *The Journey.*

- Read the sidebar on pages 75–77 of the Study Guide, and be prepared to discuss the information in reference to the lesson.
- Read and respond to the entire lesson in the Study Guide. Make note of significant things the Lord teaches you as you study.
- Pray, asking God to reveal to you the truths related to this lesson that are applicable to the class members who will attend the small-group session.

LEADING THE SMALL GROUP

Introduction: Introduce the lesson by highlighting *Think About It* on pages 73–74 in the Study Guide. Write on the board the quote at the beginning of the lesson and the Scripture verse on page 73.

Rewind: Write the following terms on the board: **Wilderness, Valley, Mountain, Desert, Detour, Oasis, Roadblock, Interstate, Rest Area, Campsite,** and any other terms applicable to the participants in the class. Ask participants to reflect on the past few months of their spiritual lives and to identify the primary term that is comparable to what they have been through. Direct them to reassemble with people who have chosen the same word as them. This will produce several small groups within the class. Be aware of anyone who is not in a group, and be prepared to join that person in the discussion. Instruct participants to discuss what they have learned about God in their recent experiences. Direct participants back to the Study Guide, and instruct them to use the activity on page 75 to identify the tools they have been given to assist them in their spiritual growth. After a brief discussion of the tools, allow the class members to return to their original seats.

Rethink: Call for participants to identify some of the tools they use in their jobs and homes. List responses on the board. Create a new list on the board, and call for participants to identify the tools they use to accomplish their spiritual tasks. Read aloud Romans 10:17. Review the verse, reading it slowly. Ask volunteers to identify what the verse means to them.

Present the following scenario: *Suppose you were on a game show and the final question required you to recite from memory as much Scripture as possible. How much could you remember?* Review the activity in which participants are asked to identify the statements that actually are in the Bible.

God helps those who help themselves (popular, but not in the Bible).

God loves a cheerful giver (2 Corinthians 9:7).

Do unto others as you would have them do unto you (Matthew 7:12).

Money is the root of all evil (not in the Bible . . . a popular misuse of 1 Timothy 6:10).

Reflect: Read aloud 2 Peter 1:19–21. Discuss what makes the Bible unique. The Bible is our guide and instructor. Call for volunteers to identify things that serve as their guides and instructors. Identify the three most influential sources in the lives of people today. Discuss why those sources are given such power.

Point out that the Bible is the standard of truth by which all other claims are evaluated. If the Bible is going to be the standard of truth today, there are some things that believers must do.

1. **Learn the Bible from others.** Read 1 Corinthians 12:27–31. List on the board the gifts Paul listed in this passage. Circle the gift of teaching, and point out that the purpose of teachers is the strengthening of the spiritual lives of believers. Use the information in the Study Guide to explain the modern examples of the words in the list of spiritual gifts. Refer to the list in the Study Guide of opportunities to learn. Highlight specific events that are available in your church and community. Read

aloud Colossians 3:12–17 and discuss the importance of learning from each other.

2. **Learn the Bible on your own.** Real conversion results in a hunger for God's Word. If you are going to learn God's Word, you must have some guidelines. Use the information in the Study Guide to lead a discussion of the following points.

   a. Come to the Bible joyfully.

   b. Come to the Bible prayerfully and expectantly.

   c. Come to the Bible systematically.

   d. Come to the Bible thoughtfully.

   e. Come to the Bible cheerfully.

React: Use the React section of the Study Guide to lead participants to discover how this lesson applies to their daily lives. Read James 1:22 and discuss the importance of hearing and doing what God says. Call for volunteers to share any particular insight they gained from this study. Remind participants to invest themselves in opportunities to learn from God's Word.

Call attention to the "Three Truths" activity at the end of the lesson. Be prepared to share your three truths as an example. Close in prayer.

LIVING AS A CHRISTIAN

CHAPTER SIX

TRAVELING TOGETHER

PREPARE TO LEAD

TO GET THE MOST FROM THIS STUDY, READ PAGES 124–133 OF *The Journey.*

- Read the sidebar on pages 94–95 of the Study Guide, and be prepared to discuss the information in reference to the lesson.
- Read and respond to the entire lesson in the Study Guide. Make note of significant things the Lord teaches you as you study.
- Pray, asking God to reveal to you the truths related to this lesson that are applicable to the class members who will attend the small-group session.

LEADING THE SMALL GROUP

Introduction: Introduce the lesson by highlighting *Think About It* on pages 91–92 in the Study Guide. Write on the board the quote at the beginning of the lesson and the Scripture verse on pages 91–92.

Rewind: Tell the story of a circus performer who performs dangerous stunts. Though the performer gets the accolades, the real heroes are those who are behind the scenes making sure that the equipment is assembled correctly and is in safe condition. Those support personnel are valuable to the circus performer; support personnel also are important to us. Call for volunteers to identify the people who are most supportive and helpful in their spiritual lives and to describe the settings in which they interact with the people listed. Discuss the difference between church membership and salvation. Point out that salvation and church membership are not the same.

Rethink: Write **Church** on the board and call for volunteers to suggest the first thing that comes to mind when they hear the word. List responses on the board. Ask: *How would you explain "church" to someone who had never heard of the concept?* Call for volunteers to respond. Direct participants to use the activity on page 96 in the Study Guide to determine what each Scripture says about the church. The following is the key to that activity:

Acts 1:8 (local group of Christians)

Acts 13:1 (local group of Christians)

1 Corinthians 1:2 (local group of Christians)

Ephesians 5:23 (the company of all believers)

Point out that the concept of the church includes both aspects—the local body or congregation and the universal body of all believers in Jesus Christ. Discuss the pros and cons of the congregational model.

Reflect: Read aloud Proverbs 27:17. Ask: *What is the role of believers in the lives of other believers?* Though it might not be a matter of discussion in your class, it is true that some people don't understand the purpose of the church in the lives of God's people. Use the information below and the information in the Study Guide to highlight four reasons believers should be involved in the local church.

1. **To worship God.** Worship isn't an hour on the church schedule; it is an attitude of grateful hearts toward the God who loves them and provides for them. Call for a volunteer to read aloud Psalm 100:4. Briefly discuss the verse and its relevance to our worship of God. Read aloud Colossians 3:16 and identify the elements that are part of worship. Ask: *How do you respond to worship styles that are different from the way you worship at your church?* Guide participants to use the activity in the Study Guide to respond to the question. Point out that God is concerned about the attitude of our hearts when we worship. Read aloud John 4:23 and discuss the kind of person God is seeking. Ask rhetorically: *Are you that kind of person?*

2. **To hear God's Word.** Read aloud Colossians 3:16 again. Ask: *What is the role of God's Word in the life of a believer?* Call attention to the question in the Study Guide regarding opportunities to engage in the study of God's Word. Ask participants to honestly evaluate their commitment to hearing God's Word.

3. **To encourage one another.** Guide participants to evaluate their recent experiences and to consider how those experiences might serve as an encouragement to others. Discuss responses. Ask: *What is the danger of seeking advice from people who are not believers?* Call for responses. Ask: *When it comes to seeking help for your problems, do you turn to fellow believers? Why or why not?* Call for responses. Read aloud Hebrews 10:25. Ask: *What is God's opinion of the importance of believers meeting together?* Call for a volunteer to read aloud Hebrews 3:13 and 1 Thessalonians 5:11. Brainstorm some small things we all can do to encourage each other. Challenge the class members to select a few of these things to do in the coming week.

4. **To reach out to others with Christ's love.** Read aloud Ephesians 4:12. Discuss some ways believers can reach out to people who are hurting or in need of God's love. List responses on the board.

React: Some people wonder how to evaluate a church before becoming a member of it. Lead a brief discussion of the points of concern that are listed in the Study Guide under the React heading. Be very cautious so as to present a positive image of your church as you discuss the way your church operates.

Call attention to the "Three Truths" activity at the end of the lesson. Be prepared to share your three truths as an example. Close in prayer.

LEAVING A LEGACY

CHAPTER ONE

THE FAMILY

PREPARE TO LEAD

TO GET THE MOST FROM THIS STUDY, READ THE PREFACE AND pages 13–18 of 267–276 of *The Journey.*

- Read the sidebar on pages 6–8 of the Study Guide, and be prepared to discuss the information in reference to the lesson.

- Read and respond to the entire lesson in the Study Guide. Make note of significant things the Lord teaches you as you study.

- Pray, asking God to reveal to you the truths related to this lesson that are applicable to the class members who will attend the small-group session.

LEADING THE SMALL GROUP

Introduction: Introduce the lesson by highlighting *Think About It* on pages 3–4 in the Study Guide. Write on the board the quote at the beginning of the lesson and the Scripture verse on pages 3–4.

Rewind: Call for volunteers to briefly describe the hopes and dreams they have for future generations. List responses on the board. Briefly discuss your childhood, and describe the amount of time you spent interacting with older relatives. Discuss with the class the importance of interacting with people who are older. Work together to identify the three things that consume the greatest portion of our everyday lives. List those activities on the board.

Ask participants what first comes to mind when they hear the word *children.* List responses on the board. Some of these probably will be humorous, so be prepared. Read aloud Genesis 33:5. Ask: *What does this verse say about raising children?* This verse tells us that children belong to God and that parents are stewards of God's possession. Ask: *How does this truth affect the way we approach child rearing?*

If possible, work through the material in the sidebar on the family. Be prepared to deal with opposing views of the family, including the nontraditional family and the idea that living together is the same as being married. This idea will be discussed in a future lesson.

Rethink: Draw a horizontal line on the board, and label the left end **Very Weak** and the right end **Very Strong**. Ask participants to use the similar activity in the

Study Guide to rate the spiritual strength of their childhood families. Then instruct them to rank their present families' strengths. Ask: *How do we account for the differences—positive and negative—between our childhood families and our present families?* Discuss responses. Ask volunteers to identify the ideal strength of their families. Brainstorm some activities that might be helpful in achieving the spiritual goals that we have for our families. List responses on the board. Direct participants to use the space provided in the Study Guide to list some personal activities that eat away at the time they have available for other people. Discuss reasons why we don't spend quality time with the younger generation.

Reflect: Write on the board: **Why does God give us children?** List responses on the board. After a few laughs, move into an explanation of the biblical reasons for being given children.

1. **God gives us children so we can prepare them to become adults.** Discuss some of the things parents do to help their children mature. Discuss the role of one's faith in this process and how parents should deal with failure in the lives of their children.

2. **God gives us children to help them develop mentally and emotionally.** Read aloud Luke 2:52, and call for volunteers to identify the three types of growth Jesus experienced. Jesus grew physically, mentally, and emotionally. Discuss some things parents can do to help their children grow in these areas. List possibilities on the board.

3. **God gives us children so we can shape their moral and spiritual character.** Call for a volunteer to read aloud Matthew 7:24–27.

Discuss the danger of a weak moral and spiritual foundation. Brainstorm some things that parents can do to prevent this from happening. Call for volunteers to identify specific things they are doing to teach their children Bible-based morality. List responses on the board. Call for a volunteer to read aloud Deuteronomy 11:19. Discuss the parental responsibility detailed in this passage. Review the list of sources of boundaries in the Study Guide, and call for participants to identify the things that are affecting the lives of them and their children.

As time permits and if your class contains parents in the child-raising years, lead a discussion of the material in the Study Guide regarding how to become a wise parent. This material can supplement the information already covered, or it can be substituted if necessary.

React: Allow the parents in the class to reflect on the joys of raising children. If there are no parents in the class, work together in small groups to develop a plan for becoming godly parents.

Call attention to the "Three Truths" activity at the end of the lesson. Be prepared to share your three truths as an example. Close in prayer.

LEAVING A LEGACY

CHAPTER TWO

MAKING AN IMPACT

PREPARE TO LEAD

TO GET THE MOST FROM THIS STUDY, READ PAGES 277–286 OF *The Journey.*

- Read the sidebar on pages 28–30 of the Study Guide, and be prepared to discuss the information in reference to the lesson.
- Read and respond to the entire lesson in the Study Guide. Make note of significant things the Lord teaches you as you study.
- Pray, asking God to reveal to you the truths related to this lesson that are applicable to the class members who will attend the small-group session.

LEADING THE SMALL GROUP

Introduction: Introduce the lesson by highlighting *Think About It* on pages 25–26 in the Study Guide. Write on the board the quote at the beginning of the lesson and the Scripture verse on pages 25–26 .

Rewind: Create a list of things people do to make a positive impact for God on the people around them. Ask: *What are some of the excuses people make for not making an impact for God?* List responses on the board. Explain that life is full of difficult tasks that people must muster up the energy to do. Included in that list of difficult tasks are some of our spiritual responsibilities. Discuss the process people go through in order to be motivated to complete difficult tasks. Ask: *Why don't we approach spiritual tasks with this degree of determination?* Call for responses.

Read aloud John 15:8. Discuss what really brings glory to God. Use the activity in the Study Guide, if necessary.

The sidebar for this lesson deals with the concept of light and how it is used in Scripture. This would make for a good alternate study or additional information for this lesson. As time allows, present this information in support of this lesson.

Rethink: Call for volunteers to share situations that have made a dramatic impact on their spiritual lives. Then discuss how God has used them to make a dramatic spiritual impact on other people. Ask: *Is it easier to remember situations in which you were the recipient or the giver? Why?* Recount the story in the Study Guide about the football kicker who refused to enter the game. Then direct participants to consider their roles in God's grand scheme—are they team players or benchwarmers? Discuss the problems associated with being unwilling to be used by God for His purposes.

Reflect: Call for a volunteer to read aloud Ephesians 1:4 and Ephesians 1:12. Discuss the application of these verses to the lives of believers. Read aloud 1 Peter 2:9 and Mark 16:15. Discuss the relevance of these verses to everyday believers, considering the fact that everything in the Bible is relevant to everyone. These verses identify basic Christian responsibilities that all believers are to fulfill. Discuss some things people do to fulfill these responsibilities. Ask: *How have you been shown God's love by other people?* Discuss responses.

Ask: *What are some things we can do to show the world God's love?* Here are some suggestions that are included in the Study Guide.

1. **Ask God to help you see the world the way He sees it.** Read aloud 2 Corinthians 5:14–16. This passage includes a portion of Paul's worldview. Compare Paul's worldview to the worldviews of people in the class, and discuss reasons people do or do not embrace Paul's worldview. Discuss reasons people don't see other people the way God sees them.

2. **Demonstrate God's love by the way you live.** Read aloud Matthew 18:6. Discuss some ways that people cause others to stumble. Be careful not to rationalize behavior that is not biblical. We cause other people to stumble when we direct them to do something that takes their attention off of God. Those are broad boundaries.

Call for a volunteer to read aloud Romans 14:12–13. Discuss Paul's perception on this subject. Make a list of "cold water" things that can be done to show other people God's love.

3. **Learn to share your faith with others.** Read aloud Romans 10:14. Discuss some practical ways to share your faith with people you know. List responses on the board. Ask participants to identify the strategies that are the most doable for them. Discuss ways they can use the strategies in their daily lives. Highlight the points to remember when sharing your faith (on page 41 of the Study Guide). Read aloud 1 Peter 3:15 and discuss the fact that believers should always be ready to share their faith with nonbelievers.

4. **Pray for the opportunity to share God's love with others and for the willingness for others to hear God's voice.** Read aloud Colossians 4:3, then identify three people with whom individuals can pray regarding their desire to share their faith.

React: Read aloud Luke 10:2 and discuss the urgency to share our faith with people who do not know Christ. Ask volunteers to identify people who were willing to share their faith with them. Lead the class to commit to being the kind of people who willingly and gladly share their faith during every opportunity they get.

Call attention to the "Three Truths" activity at the end of the lesson. Be prepared to share your three truths as an example. Close in prayer.

LEAVING A LEGACY

CHAPTER THREE

AS LIFE MOVES ON

PREPARE TO LEAD

TO GET THE MOST FROM THIS STUDY, READ PAGES 287–292 OF *The Journey.*

- Read the sidebar on pages 52–54 of the Study Guide, and be prepared to discuss the information in reference to the lesson.
- Read and respond to the entire lesson in the Study Guide. Make note of significant things the Lord teaches you as you study.
- Pray, asking God to reveal to you the truths related to this lesson that are applicable to the class members who will attend the small-group session.

LEADING THE SMALL GROUP

Introduction: Introduce the lesson by highlighting *Think About It* on pages 49–50 in the Study Guide. Write on the board the quote at the beginning of the lesson and the Scripture verse on pages 49–50.

Rewind: Call for volunteers to share some of their spiritual highs and lows. List responses in two columns on the board. Briefly go through the responses to the multiple-choice question that asks them to describe their spiritual journeys.

Briefly describe the life of King Saul who, though anointed by God as king, abandoned his spiritual roots in order to pursue selfish gain. Use the sidebar on the life of Saul for more information related to his background and life as Israel's king. Ask someone to describe how he or she has been affected by the same things that affected Saul. Be prepared to share your own story.

Rethink: Call for volunteers to suggest things that might be the biggest threats to their spiritual growth. List responses on the board. Work through the list identifying ways that believers can be strengthened against the threats. Arrange the class into six small groups, and assign each group one decade to consider (20s, 30s, 40s, 50s, 60s, and 70+). Instruct groups to identify the most significant challenges facing people in each decade. After a few minutes, call for groups to report their findings. List responses on the board.

Reflect: One of the greatest challenges that accompanies aging is the empty nest. For adults who have children, this is a stark reality; for those who don't have children, this is great advice in advance. No matter what the relationship, these words are great advice.

1. **Beware of marital discord.** Call for volunteers to read aloud Genesis 2:24; Matthew 5:32; and, Mark 10:9. Discuss the biblical picture of marriage as presented by these verses. Review the list of suggested relationship-building activities and call for volunteers to share other activities that they have found helpful.

2. **Don't be preoccupied with other things.** Call for a volunteer to suggest some things that might become objects of their preoccupation and then identify some ways to prevent someone from becoming preoccupied with outside interests or anything that interferes with the marital relationship. Lead a brief discussion of 1 Corinthians 13. If time allows, call for a volunteer to read aloud the passage. Discuss the relationship of this passage to the marriage relationship and to dealing with marital transitions, such as the empty nest.

3. **Protect your relationship with God.** Call for volunteers to read the following passages: 1 Samuel 9:17; 1 Samuel 13:13–14; 1 Samuel 15:10–11; and 1 Samuel 15:24–29. Draw a horizontal line on the board and list a summary of Saul's relationship with God along the line. Point out that it was never Saul's plan to be distanced from God and eventually rejected by God. Discuss some of the things that might have caused Saul to drift away from his relationship with God. Call for volunteers to suggest some things that can be done to protect our relationships with God. Make sure to call attention to spiritual growth opportunities presented by your church.

React: Point out that many believers agree with God's Word until it challenges them in a specific area of life. Discuss the possible responses to being challenged to change a thought, behavior, or belief. List responses on the board. It is important that believers let God's Word challenge them in their thoughts, beliefs, and actions . . . especially in the area of marriage. Be careful not to sidestep the difficult passages of the Bible or the ones that remind people that eternity will be spent in one of two places—heaven or hell. Embracing any philosophy—no matter how popular—that minimizes personal accountability will take them on a spiritual detour.

Call attention to the "Three Truths" activity at the end of the lesson. Be prepared to share your three truths as an example. Close in prayer.

LEAVING A LEGACY

CHAPTER FOUR

RETIREMENT: A NEW BEGINNING

PREPARE TO LEAD

TO GET THE MOST FROM THIS STUDY, READ PAGES 293–297 OF *The Journey.*

- Read the sidebar on pages 72–73 of the Study Guide, and be prepared to discuss the information in reference to the lesson.
- Read and respond to the entire lesson in the Study Guide. Make note of significant things the Lord teaches you as you study.
- Pray, asking God to reveal to you the truths related to this lesson that are applicable to the class members who will attend the small-group session.

LEADING THE SMALL GROUP

Introduction: Introduce the lesson by highlighting *Think About It* on pages 69–70 in the Study Guide. Write on the board the quote at the beginning of the lesson and the Scripture verse on page 69.

Rewind: Write **Retirement** on the board, and ask participants to give their first thoughts about the idea of retirement. List responses on the board. Call for volunteers to suggest synonyms for retirement. List those responses on the board. Read aloud Genesis 2:15 and Genesis 3:17–19. Discuss how the concept of retirement relates to these terms.

The sidebar in this lesson raises the concept of older individuals in society. If the class setting is appropriate, take the time to work through the sidebar as an addition to the lesson content.

Rethink: Ask: *Is retirement a beginning or an end?* Call for responses. Discuss what people might do if they retired tomorrow. List responses on the board. Discuss each possibility, asking if it actually is their real desire of life or just something to do. Arrange the class in small groups, and instruct each group to discuss their responses to the question: *What would you do with your life if money was not an object?* After a few moments, call for responses. Consider the focus of the answers to the previous question. Are people in the class primarily concerned with doing something that will benefit society or benefit themselves? Discuss responses.

When considering retirement, people consider a variety of life issues, including their spiritual, financial, emotional, and spiritual health. Discuss different ways people prepare for retirement in these areas. In which areas are people directing their efforts? If all of one's efforts are focused in one area, what is the effect on the other areas? Discuss responses.

Reflect: Call for a volunteer to read aloud Matthew 28:20. Identify in this passage Jesus' plans for our lives. Point out that Jesus doesn't want our lives to be frustrating; He wants them to be used for His glory. That is where we find our greatest satisfaction in life. But what can we do to stay focused throughout life? Lead a discussion of the following points:

1. **Be alert to the dangers.** Like King David discovered, no one is immune to temptation. Call for volunteers to identify some of the dangers that godly people face every day. List responses on the board. Discuss some things people can do to guard themselves against these temptations. Call for a volunteer to read aloud Proverbs 4:23. Discuss some ways this verse can become a reality in our lives.

2. **Strengthen your commitment to Christ.** Read Proverbs 10:9. Ask participants to identify the end result of a growing relationship with God. List responses on the board, making sure that integrity is on the list. If integrity isn't on the list, add it and discuss how God's character naturally produces personal integrity.

3. **Commit every situation to God, and trust Him for the outcome.** Call for participants to reflect on the fears they have at the moment and to evaluate their personal anxiety. Call for a volunteer to read aloud Isaiah 26:4. Ask: *What does this verse say about our fears?* Call for responses.

4. **Strengthen the relationships God already has given you.** Direct participants to identify the primary relationships they have in their lives and to evaluate the strength of those relationships. Call for volunteers to suggest ways they can strengthen their relationships. List responses on the board. Point out that Satan attacks people when they are alone and in the areas of their greatest weaknesses. Pray that God will make us aware of Satan's attacks so that we will not do anything that will discredit God and our commitment to Him.

React: Call for a volunteer to read aloud 2 Timothy 4:7. Discuss what might make this statement true about each of us. Point out that finishing well means being willing to admit when you are weak and being willing to help others when you are strong. Identify ministries in your church that can strengthen believers for their long-term spiritual benefit.

Call attention to the "Three Truths" activity at the end of the lesson. Be prepared to share your three truths as an example. Close in prayer.

LEAVING A LEGACY

CHAPTER FIVE

OUR FINAL DESTINATION

PREPARE TO LEAD

TO GET THE MOST FROM THIS STUDY, READ PAGES 298–302 of *The Journey.*

- Read the sidebar on pages 95–97 of the Study Guide, and be prepared to discuss the information in reference to the lesson.
- Read and respond to the entire lesson in the Study Guide. Make note of significant things the Lord teaches you as you study.
- Pray, asking God to reveal to you the truths related to this lesson that are applicable to the class members who will attend the small-group session.

LEADING THE SMALL GROUP

Introduction: Introduce the lesson by highlighting *Think About It* on pages 91–92 in the Study Guide. Write on the board the quote at the beginning of the lesson and the Scripture verse on pages 91–92 .

Rewind: Call for a volunteer to read aloud Job 14:1–2, 10. Write **Death** on the board and ask: *Is this the beginning or the end?* Call for responses. Point out that in light of eternity, death is the beginning of the biggest part of our existence. Our life on earth is simply a small bit of time. Read aloud 1 Corinthians 2:9–10, then call for volunteers to suggest some paraphrases for the passage. Write on the board: **I enjoy . . .** Then call for volunteers to suggest completions to the statement. List responses on the board. Then ask people how they stay motivated to perform the tasks. Point out that heaven is something we will definitely enjoy, and the realization of it should be motivation for us to keep serving and pleasing God.

If your class is deeper spiritually, you might consider expanding the study to include the information on heaven in the sidebar. Use the information there to enrich the study of this lesson, or revisit the sidebar at some point in the future.

Rethink: Write **Heaven** on the board. Call for volunteers to describe what they believe heaven will be like. Assign the following Scriptures to volunteers to read aloud: Deuteronomy 26:15; Revelation 21:11; and Revelation 21:21. Instruct participants to listen to each verse and to note what each verse says about heaven. Sometimes we focus on the physical aspects of heaven rather than the experience of heaven. It's not important what it will be like visually; it's very important that we understand how our lives will be lived out there.

Write **Hell** on the board and call for volunteers to describe what hell might be like. Ask volunteers to suggest some misconceptions about hell that they have heard. Hell will be the ultimate in isolation—eternal punishment and no one to feel sorry for you. Discuss reasons people might knowingly reject Christ and choose eternity in hell. Arrange the class in pairs, and ask them to identify how they would respond to someone who is comfortable with spending eternity in hell. After a few moments, call for volunteers to report their thoughts.

Reflect: Read aloud Philippians 3:20. Write on the board: **When** and **If**. Ask participants to determine which word best represents their certainty about spending eternity in heaven. Suggest that anyone who wonders if he or she will be in heaven should speak with you after class. Arrange the class in small groups or pairs, and ask them to consider the privileges of citizenship in heaven. Instruct them to use the Study Guide to record their thoughts. Call for groups to report their responses as you list them on the board. Then instruct the groups to consider what might be some of the responsibilities of citizenship in heaven. Call for and list those responses on the board. Ask participants to consider which we are more aware of—privileges or responsibilities. Point out that Paul was motivated to ministry by the reality that he would spend eternity in heaven with God.

Direct participants to reflect on some of the trials they face in life and to record them in the space provided in the Study Guide. Call for volunteers to identify how a focus on citizenship in heaven can help us deal with today's trials.

Call for a volunteer to read aloud 2 Corinthians 11:22–27. List on the board the dangers Paul faced while serving God. Then ask how many people in the room have suffered one of the dangers listed on the board. Then ask how many have suffered two or more. Point out that Paul faced incredible obstacles but remained faithful to his calling to share Christ with everyone he met.

Call for a volunteer to read aloud Ephesians 2:19–22, then discuss the following permanent changes brought about by salvation. Use the material in the Study Guide to supplement your discussion.

1. **We become members of God's household** (v. 19).
2. **We gain a partnership with the giants of the faith who have preceded us** (v. 20).
3. **We become the temple of God** (vv. 21–22).

React: Call for a volunteer to read aloud 1 Corinthians 15:51–58. Use this passage as a backdrop for a discussion of the biblical view of death. Point out that death is inevitable for everyone. No one will live on this earth forever. The greater concern today is not this life, but the next life—the eternal life. Call for participants to list the names of people they know who do not know Christ in the space provided in the Study Guide. Lead participants to commit to pray for and speak with these people as soon as possible.

Call attention to the "Three Truths" activity at the end of the lesson. Be prepared to share your three truths as an example. Close in prayer.

LEAVING A LEGACY

CHAPTER SIX

HOME AT LAST

PREPARE TO LEAD

To get the most from this study, read pages 303–309 of *The Journey.*

- Read the sidebar on pages 117–118 of the Study Guide, and be prepared to discuss the information in reference to the lesson.
- Read and respond to the entire lesson in the Study Guide. Make note of significant things the Lord teaches you as you study.
- Pray, asking God to reveal to you the truths related to this lesson that are applicable to the class members who will attend the small-group session.

LEADING THE SMALL GROUP

Introduction: Introduce the lesson by highlighting *Think About It* on pages 113–114 in the Study Guide. Write on the board the quote at the beginning of the lesson and the Scripture verse on pages 113–114.

Rewind: Ask: *What are some things people do to earn a place in heaven?* List responses on the board. Discuss the validity of the activities listed. Point out that there is nothing we can do in the way of good works to gain access to heaven. Heaven is a "by invitation only" place. Lead a discussion about the afterlife and what we believe it will be like. Use information in the Study Guide and in the book to provide background information. Write **Spiritual** and **Physical** on the board. Ask participants to discuss these two concepts in relation to death. Ask: *Which one is more important today? Which one will be more important later in life?* If time allows, discuss the importance of the ancient pyramids in Egypt (use the sidebar on pages 116–117 for information related to this subject).

Rethink: Ask: *How do you know if heaven is real or not? How do you know if you will go to heaven when you die?* Call for responses. Make sure there is no confusion about the issue of going to heaven. Point out that entrance to heaven is only possible through faith in Jesus Christ. There is no other way to enter heaven. Point out that "faith" means more than simple belief; it means trusting Christ and what He has done for us for our eternal salvation.

Reflect: Amidst all of the confusion about heaven, there are four truths we must keep in mind. These truths are biblical and, therefore, can't be disputed.

1. **In heaven, we will be with God.** Call for a volunteer to read aloud 1 Thessalonians 4:17. Point out Paul's description of heaven. Describe heaven as a place where there will be no more evil, sorrow, suffering, pain, illness, or problems. Read aloud Revelation 21:3–4, calling attention to the descriptive words used to describe heaven in terms that we can understand. Call for participants to suggest reasons people might choose not to be in a place where they will be with God. List responses on the board, highlighting the fact that most people would choose to avoid being in God's presence because of spiritual reasons.

2. **In heaven, we will be home.** Write **Home** on the board, and ask volunteers to suggest characteristics of home. Keep in mind that some people have negative concepts of home because their early years were less than positive. Ask volunteers to read aloud Hebrews 11:13 and Philippians 3:20. Discuss the biblical concept of home as related to the ideas listed on the board. Point out any similarities or differences. Remind participants that we were initially created to be in paradise with God. In going to heaven, we will return to that place for which we were originally designed.

3. **In heaven, we will be like Christ.** Call for volunteers to suggest characteristics of Jesus. List responses on the board. Discuss some of the characteristics of Christ that are difficult for humans to possess. Call for a volunteer to read aloud 1 Corinthians 15:51–52. Call attention to the changes that take place when a person goes to heaven. Consider the physical changes and the spiritual changes.

In going to heaven, we will experience a change in nature—we will no longer naturally rebel against God; we will please Him. Sin will be erased from our presence, and we will live in perfect harmony with God. Direct participants to use the Study Guide to write a personal paraphrase of 1 John 3:2 as a prayer of thanksgiving. Call for volunteers to share their prayers with the class.

4. **In heaven, we will be part of a new creation.** Call for volunteers to share examples of the decaying nature of our world. Point out that things aren't getting better; they are getting worse. Call for volunteers to read aloud Romans 8:21 and Isaiah 11:6. Lead a discussion of the characteristics of heaven that are different from the world in which we live.

One of the most common questions in Christian circles concerns the timing of Christ's return. Many people have tried to predict the timing, but doing so violates the biblical revelation. Call for a volunteer to read aloud 2 Peter 3:10–13. Ask: *According to this passage, when will Christ return? What will happen when He returns?* Call for responses. If time allows, use the additional material in the Study Guide to lead a more in-depth study of this concept.

React: Heaven and hell are real places and are our only two options for living in eternity. Read aloud Romans 8:1, and point out that heaven is open to everyone who will choose to live in a right relationship with Jesus Christ. Lead the class to conclude this lesson using the interactive elements in the *React* section of the Study Guide.

Call attention to the "Three Truths" activity at the end of the lesson. Be prepared to share your three truths as an example. Close in prayer.

DEALING WITH DOUBT

CHAPTER ONE

CAN WE BE SURE?

PREPARE TO LEAD

TO GET THE MOST FROM THIS STUDY, READ THE PREFACE AND pages 63–67 of *The Journey.*

- Read the sidebar on pages 6–7 of the Study Guide, and be prepared to discuss the information in reference to the lesson.
- Read and respond to the entire lesson in the Study Guide. Make note of significant things the Lord teaches you as you study.
- Pray, asking God to reveal to you the truths related to this lesson that are applicable to the class members who will attend the small-group session.

LEADING THE SMALL GROUP

Introduction: Introduce the lesson by highlighting *Think About It* on pages 3–4 in the Study Guide. Write on the board the quote at the beginning of the lesson and the Scripture verse on page 3.

Rewind: Arrange the class in pairs or in small groups, and instruct participants to discuss things they expected God to do but He didn't do. Allow a few minutes for the discussion, then call for volunteers to report. As participants respond, ask them to report how their faith was affected by the situations they described. Call attention to the Study Guide, and ask participants to identify the mistakes they made in the situations in which they felt they were let down by God.

Show a collection of recent newspapers, pointing out that most of the headlines are negative, or highlight something that should be of concern. Ask: *How is it possible in today's world to trust God and to believe He will keep His promises?* Discuss responses. If the class is comprised of people who might understand the concept of "backsliding," lead a discussion of the concept using the material in the sidebar in the Study Guide. If you do not use the sidebar, you might consider using it at some point in an upcoming class session.

Rethink: Ask: *Why do people question their faith or their salvation?* List responses on the board. Some possible responses are "I don't feel saved" and "I don't see anything happening in my spiritual life." Call for participants to suggest some things that happen to people's spiritual lives when they begin to doubt their faith or salvation. Point out that causing people to doubt their salvation or their faith is one of Satan's most effective weapons against believers.

Reflect: Refer to the list of reasons people doubt their faith or their salvation as you identify the general reasons for such thoughts. Assign each reason listed on the board to one of the categories in the following list of reasons people doubt their faith.

1. **We doubt our salvation because we still sin and fear God will reject us because of it.** No one is unaffected by personal sin. Therefore, we can always feel unworthy of God's love. We naturally disappoint God and can feel unloved and rejected. This is something Satan wants us to feel. Call for volunteers to suggest how they respond when someone disappoints them. List responses on the board. Point out that it is easy to assign these actions to God because this is the way we respond. But the Bible tells us that God's ways and our ways are not the same. Read aloud Psalm 145:8, calling attention to the way in which God responds when we disappoint Him. Ask: *What happens when we expect other Christians to be perfect?* Discuss responses.

2. **We doubt our salvation because we depend solely on our emotions.** Read aloud Ephesians 4:14. Discuss the problems associated with basing one's faith on his or her emotions. Call for volunteers to report times when they based their feelings about their salvation on their emotions. Ask them to describe how their emotions affected their faith. Draw on the board a line that represents the normal spiritual life—high peaks and low valleys. Then draw a dashed line through the middle of the first line. Point out that people "feel" saved when they are living above the dashed line and don't "feel" saved when they are below it. Yet we know that God's love is permanent.

Therefore, believing that we aren't saved after we know we are is the same as suggesting that God's Word isn't true or that God is a liar. If God said His love is permanent, then it is permanent, or He is lying. Which one is more believable?

3. **We also doubt our salvation because of misguided humility.** Some people discredit their spiritual lives by claiming that they don't deserve salvation. That is true, but deserve it or not, salvation is a gift—something God provides to those who receive it. Call for a volunteer to read aloud Ephesians 2:8–9. This familiar passage points out that salvation is 100 percent God and zero percent us—it is not something we deserve. Review the passage, highlighting the requirements for salvation.

Arrange the class in small groups or pairs, and instruct participants to discuss what they learned about God and about themselves when they experienced salvation. Suggest that they record their responses in the space provided in the Study Guide. Review the facts about Jesus on page 12 in the Study Guide.

React: Use the material in the React section of the Study Guide to frame the conclusion of the lesson. Call for volunteers to briefly share about the first time they asked Jesus Christ into their lives. Be sure to focus on what God is doing right now rather than paying too much attention to what God did several years ago. The idea is to present Jesus as relevant to the present, not a person in the past.

Call attention to the "Three Truths" activity at the end of the lesson. Be prepared to share your three truths as an example. Close in prayer.

DEALING WITH DOUBT

CHAPTER TWO

OUR FIRM FOUNDATION

PREPARE TO LEAD

TO GET THE MOST FROM THIS STUDY, READ PAGES 67–73 OF *The Journey.*

- Read the sidebar on pages 21–22 of the Study Guide, and be prepared to discuss the information in reference to the lesson.

- Read and respond to the entire lesson in the Study Guide. Make note of significant things the Lord teaches you as you study.

- Pray, asking God to reveal to you the truths related to this lesson that are applicable to the class members who will attend the small-group session.

LEADING THE SMALL GROUP

Introduction: Introduce the lesson by highlighting *Think About It* on pages 19–20 in the Study Guide. Write on the board the quote at the beginning of the lesson and the Scripture verse on pages 19–20.

Rewind: Write **Facts** on the board, and call for volunteers to identify some nonnegotiable facts about their faith. List responses on the board. For each fact, call for volunteers to suggest why it is nonnegotiable. Ask: *Upon what evidence are these facts based?* Review the information in the sidebar on "promises" and, if time allows, include this information in your presentation of the material in this lesson.

Rethink: Call for volunteers to identify situations in which their faith was at its highest and times when it was at its lowest. Discuss the circumstances that surrounded those highs and lows. Call for a volunteer to read aloud Psalm 62:7. Ask participants to reflect on the truthfulness of this statement as related to their lives. Write on the board: **When times get tough, my faith . . .** Call for volunteers to complete the statement, referencing real-life situations in their lives. Direct participants to the activity in the Study Guide, and instruct them to select the response that best represents the role of their faith in difficult circumstances.

Reflect: Ask: *Upon what do you base your faith in God?* Explain that God has given us some foundational facts upon which to rely when life gets tough.

1. **The rock of God's promises.** Ask participants to identify some of the reasons it is so difficult for us to trust people. List responses on the

board. Ask if any of these reasons are ever applied to God so that we don't trust Him as we should. Discuss responses. Call for a volunteer to read aloud Psalm 18:30. Ask participants to decide if this verse is true or false. Ask: *If it is true, then how are we to respond to everything God has said?* Call for responses. Point out that if the verse is untrue, then nothing in Scripture can be trusted.

Direct participants to read Malachi 3:6 and to complete the fill-in-the-blank activity in the Study Guide. Point out that God's ways of dealing with His people are consistent throughout Scripture. Call for volunteers to read aloud Romans 8:38–39 and John 10:28. Based on these verses, we can be certain that our salvation is secure. Write on the board: **God's promises are true; it's His character.**

2. **The rock of Christ's finished work.** Read aloud John 19:30. Ask: *What did Jesus finish? Was it His life? Was it His work?* Jesus finished what He was intended to do—bring salvation to the world. Read Luke 19:10 and call for participants to identify Jesus' purpose in coming to the world. Though Jesus died, the real significance is found in His resurrection.

Arrange the class in four groups, and assign each group one of the following passages to read. Their purpose is to identify what their passage says about Jesus Christ: Matthew 27:59–60; Matthew 27:66; Matthew 28:2; and Matthew 28:9–10.

You can't do anything to make your salvation more secure; salvation depends on what Jesus Christ has done for us.

3. **The rock of the Spirit's witness.** Ask participants to relate how they feel to the security of their salvation. Ask: *Is there any connection?* Read aloud Romans 8:16 and 2 Corinthians 1:22, and discuss the role of the Holy Spirit in salvation. Instruct participants to use the activity in the Study Guide to rate their attitudes, thoughts, behaviors, desires, and priorities. Ask: *What difference should the Holy Spirit make in the lives of believers?* Call for responses. Read aloud 1 John 3:6 and identify the one effect of the Holy Spirit on the lives of believers. Ask: *Do you have a decreasing desire to sin?* If not, then you are preventing the Holy Spirit's work in your life.

React: Write **Doubts** on the board. Ask participants to reflect on the validity of their doubts based on the Scripture in this lesson. Challenge participants to commit to memory the verses suggested in the Study Guide. Review the information in the Study Guide as you bring the lesson to a close.

Call attention to the "Three Truths" activity at the end of the lesson. Be prepared to share your three truths as an example. Close in prayer.

DEALING WITH DOUBT

CHAPTER THREE

THE UNENDING BATTLE

PREPARE TO LEAD

TO GET THE MOST FROM THIS STUDY, READ PAGES 94–103 OF *The Journey.*

- Read the sidebar on pages 40–41 of the Study Guide, and be prepared to discuss the information in reference to the lesson.

- Read and respond to the entire lesson in the Study Guide. Make note of significant things the Lord teaches you as you study.

- Pray, asking God to reveal to you the truths related to this lesson that are applicable to the class members who will attend the small-group session.

LEADING THE SMALL GROUP

Introduction: Introduce the lesson by highlighting *Think About It* on pages 37–38 in the Study Guide. Write on the board the quote at the beginning of the lesson and the Scripture verse on page 37.

Rewind: Call for volunteers to detail some times when their plans were redirected by something unexpected. Don't spend too much time on this activity; the point is to prove that our plans often are redirected unexpectedly. Review the types of prayers listed in the Study Guide, and discuss how each type of prayer might have sounded in one or more of the situations discussed. Ask: *Does becoming a Christian make us immune to problems in our lives?* Discuss responses. Direct participants to use the activity in the Study Guide to evaluate their most recent major problem. Reflect on the three responses provided in the Study Guide. The sidebar for this lesson is on miracles. If time allows, consider the concept of miracles in light of everyday life. Avoid getting sidetracked, however, by this topic.

Rethink: Direct participants to use the activity in the Study Guide to identify their greatest desires in life. Call for a volunteer to read aloud John 14:27. Point out that Jesus left us with peace, not the other things on the list. Discuss the importance of peace as it relates to dealing with the everyday issues of life. Use the information in the Study Guide to lead a discussion of the three kinds of peace mentioned in the book.

1. *Peace with God.* Read aloud Romans 5:1, and call attention to the fact that we can be at peace with God.

2. *Peace in our hearts.* Read aloud Philippians 4:6–7. Ask: *What is the difference between living with a sense of gratitude rather than with a sense of dread?* Discuss responses. This is the kind of peace God provides when we are at peace with Him.

3. *Peace with others.* Read aloud Romans 12:18. Once we experience personal peace, we can be at peace with others because we know how much God loves them and wants to be at peace with them, too.

Ask: *What are some things people try in their search for peace?* List responses on the board. Using the activity in the Study Guide, discuss what a person's level of peace reveals about his or her relationship with God. Allow time for participants to reflect on their plan for achieving peace with God.

Reflect: We all deal with spiritual warfare, in which Satan wants to distract us with spiritual untruths. Three of those untruths are part of this lesson. Review each untruth and the Scripture that debunks it.

1. **Evil isn't real.** Arrange the class in small groups or in pairs, and ask them to discuss their responses to the activities in the Study Guide. Call for volunteers to suggest ways they know evil is real. List responses on the board. Review the choices in response to the question, "What determines right and wrong for you?"

2. **Evil is real, but we'll never be able to overcome it.** Ask participants to reflect on reasons why people might believe that the battle between good and evil can't be won by God. Call for a volunteer to

read aloud Colossians 2:15, and discuss the battle between God and Satan.

3. **Evil is real, but I must fight it on my own.** If possible, share a situation you faced in which you had the opportunity to give a situation to God, but you chose to fight it yourself first. Point out that our strength for the battle is our relationship with Jesus Christ. Direct participants to complete the activity in the Study Guide in which they are asked to determine their preparation for the battle. Call for a volunteer to read aloud Zephaniah 3:17. Discuss the relevance of this verse to the spiritual battles we face.

Read aloud James 4:7–8 and complete the acrostic in the Study Guide. Discuss what it means to submit to God, making sure to point out that it doesn't mean being selective about the areas in which we are obedient. Direct participants to write personal paraphrases of Psalm 144:2 in the space provided in the Study Guide. Call for volunteers to share their paraphrases.

React: Point to the need for people to be in relationships with God, using the material in the React section of the Study Guide to lead the discussion. Pay particular attention to the list of things that should be part of a person's spiritual life.

Call attention to the "Three Truths" activity at the end of the lesson. Be prepared to share your three truths as an example. Close in prayer.

DEALING WITH DOUBT

CHAPTER FOUR

OUR CONSTANT HELPER

PREPARE TO LEAD

TO GET THE MOST FROM THIS STUDY, READ PAGES 134–142 OF *The Journey.*

- Read the sidebar on pages 58–59 of the Study Guide, and be prepared to discuss the information in reference to the lesson.
- Read and respond to the entire lesson in the Study Guide. Make note of significant things the Lord teaches you as you study.
- Pray, asking God to reveal to you the truths related to this lesson that are applicable to the class members who will attend the small-group session.

LEADING THE SMALL GROUP

Introduction: Introduce the lesson by highlighting *Think About It* on pages 55–56 in the Study Guide. Write on the board the quote at the beginning of the lesson and the Scripture verse on page 55.

Rewind: Arrange the class in small groups or pairs, and ask them to discuss their responses to the question, "If the Holy Spirit had free reign in your life, what would change?" After a few minutes, call for individuals to share some areas of their lives that would be transformed. Discuss some of the reasons people don't give God full control of their lives. List responses on the board. Call for a volunteer to read aloud John 14:16–17. Discuss the conditions of the promise Jesus made in this passage. Read aloud Romans 8:9, pointing out that at salvation, the Holy Spirit permanently moves inside all believers. If time allows, use the sidebar to lead a discussion of one of the most controversial topics in Christianity—the Trinity.

Rethink: Ask participants to identify their two greatest needs in life, using the list provided in the activity in the Study Guide. Point out that the two primary spiritual needs in life are forgiveness and goodness. Call for a volunteer to read aloud Romans 7:18–19. Ask participants to reflect on the application of Paul's words to their lives. Call for volunteers to share stories about times when they trusted their own abilities rather than relying on the Holy Spirit. Ask them to briefly describe the outcome of those situations. Ask them to project how things might have been different if they had relied on the Holy Spirit.

Reflect: Write the following question on the board: **Who is the Holy Spirit?** Direct participants to use the activity in the Study Guide to respond to the question. Transition into a biblical description of the Holy Spirit, pointing out that the Bible tells us three things about the Holy Spirit.

1. **The Holy Spirit is a person**. Read aloud Romans 8:16 and discuss what it says about the Holy Spirit. Point out that the Holy Spirit has all of the attributes of God, and He is not an impersonal force, but a person. List some of the following attributes on the board: He speaks to us, instructs us, intercedes for us, hears us, and guides us. These all are personal characteristics.

2. **The Holy Spirit is a power.** Call for volunteers to read aloud the following verses. As each verse is read, identify what each one says about the activity of the Holy Spirit: Genesis 1:2; Job 33:4; Judges 15:14; and Exodus 31:3. Direct participants to use the activity in the Study Guide to match the Scripture passages with the messages. The correct responses are:

   a. Isaiah 55:11—God's Word will accomplish its purpose.

   b. John 3:6—The Spirit produces spiritual change.

   c. 2 Corinthians 1:22—The Spirit guarantees the future.

3. **The Holy Spirit is God.** The Holy Spirit isn't an additional aspect of God; the Holy Spirit is God. Read aloud 2 Corinthians 3:17 and discuss what the verse says about God. The more the Holy Spirit lives through us, the more we develop God's perspective on every aspect of

life. When we aren't giving the Holy Spirit control, we as believers will not demonstrate godliness in our lives.

Call for volunteers to read aloud the following Scriptures, then discuss what each one says about the work of the Holy Spirit: John 16:8; John 16:13; and Acts 1:8. Direct participants to use the activity in the Study Guide to evaluate their satisfaction with their spiritual lives and to identify possible reasons for any degree of dissatisfaction.

React: As you close the lesson, call for participants to reflect on their honest responses to the following questions:

1. *Are you allowing God to convict you of sin?* Point out that it is the work of the Holy Spirit to convict people of sin.
2. *Are you allowing the Holy Spirit to teach and guide you?* Call for volunteers to identify some of the spiritual lessons they have learned in the past seven days and to identify the settings in which they learned the lessons.
3. *Are you telling others about Christ?* Point out that telling people about Christ isn't an assignment for the spiritually elite; it is an assignment for everyone. Discuss reasons people don't share their faith, and lead participants to list some people with whom they should be sharing their faith.

Call attention to the "Three Truths" activity at the end of the lesson. Be prepared to share your three truths as an example. Close in prayer.

DEALING WITH DOUBT

CHAPTER FIVE

STRENGTH FOR EACH DAY

PREPARE TO LEAD

TO GET THE MOST FROM THIS STUDY, READ PAGES 143–152 OF *The Journey.*

- Read the sidebar on pages 76–77 of the Study Guide, and be prepared to discuss the information in reference to the lesson.
- Read and respond to the entire lesson in the Study Guide. Make note of significant things the Lord teaches you as you study.
- Pray, asking God to reveal to you the truths related to this lesson that are applicable to the class members who will attend the small-group session.

LEADING THE SMALL GROUP

Introduction: Introduce the lesson by highlighting *Think About It* on pages 73–74 in the Study Guide. Write on the board the quote at the beginning of the lesson and the Scripture verse on page 73.

Rewind: Ask participants to identify some of the sources of help they seek when facing a problem. Write responses on the board. If not mentioned, add **God** to the list. Ask them to reflect on situations in which they turned to God after having exhausted all other options. Discuss how things might have been different if they had turned to God first instead of last.

Enlist a volunteer to read aloud Luke 8:1–15. As the passage is read, list the different types of soil described in the parable: wayside soil, rocky soil, thorny soil, and fertile soil. Briefly describe how individuals representing each type of soil respond to God's Word and His direction in their lives. Call for participants to use the Study Guide to identify the types of soil that represent their spiritual lives.

The sidebar for this lesson is on tribulation. This material can be supplemental to the lesson, or it can be used as an alternate lesson at a future date. Review the information to determine how it best meets the needs of your class.

Rethink: Write **Goal** on the board, and call for volunteers to suggest some of the goals they have for their lives. List responses on the board. Then write on the board: **God's goal**. Ask volunteers to identify God's goals for their lives. List responses on the board. Review the two lists, pointing out any similarities and differences. Ask: *What happens when our goals and God's goals don't match?* Call for responses.

Call for volunteers to read aloud the following Scriptures: 2 Corinthians 3:18; Galatians 4:19; and 1 John 3:2. Draw a horizontal line on the board and label the left point **Without God in My Life** and the right point **Just Like God**. Use the line to illustrate the fact that we all begin at the far left and move toward the right. This process of becoming more like God is called discipleship. Read aloud Philippians 2:15 and discuss its application to the concept of discipleship.

Arrange the class in pairs or in small groups, and instruct them to use the Study Guide to identify how they spend their leisure time. After a few moments, review the list of activities and identify the spiritual value of each activity.

Reflect: Write the following words on the board: **Character**, **Actions**, and **Attitudes**. Point out that God's desire is to conform each of these areas to His image. Discuss what prevents us from showing godly character, actions, and attitudes. List responses on the board. Use the material in the Study Guide to lead a discussion of these concepts before proceeding to the strategy for changing them to conform to God's expectations.

How can we change our lives so that our character, actions, and attitudes are in line with God's? Here is the process to follow:

1. **Repent.** Read aloud Psalm 139:23–24, and identify all of the areas of our lives that are hidden from God. Of course, there is nothing God doesn't know. Point out that God's knowing everything about us necessitates our willingness to repent and agree with God about our sins.

2. **Submit.** Ask volunteers to identify the differences between knowing what to do and actually doing it. Ask: *Which is easier?* Point out that Satan doesn't care what we know as long as we don't do it. Call for volunteers to read the following Scriptures: Luke 9:23; Colossians 3:5; Galatians 2:20; and Ephesians 4:22–24. Discuss the instructions in each passage referencing the concept of submitting to God's plan. Read aloud James 4:7–8 and challenge participants to make this passage part of the theme for their lives.

3. **Obey.** Obedience to God is never a bad choice. Knowing what God wants us to do isn't as difficult as we believe it to be. Most of the things God wants us to do are identified in Scripture. God will never tell us to do anything that violates the principles of Scripture. When we consider these facts, our confusion can be minimized. Read aloud Psalm 119:101, calling attention to the purpose of God's Word in our lives.

React: Call for a volunteer to read aloud Galatians 5:22–23. Direct participants to use the activity in the Study Guide to rank their lives in regard to the fruit of the Spirit as described in the Galatians passage. Growing in our faith is something that we must be intentional about doing. If we don't make it a priority, we will choose to do things that interfere with that desire in our lives. Use the remaining time to work through the React section of the Study Guide before bringing the class to a close.

Call attention to the "Three Truths" activity at the end of the lesson. Be prepared to share your three truths as an example. Close in prayer.

DEALING WITH DOUBT

CHAPTER SIX

SUFFERING AND LOSS

PREPARE TO LEAD

TO GET THE MOST FROM THIS STUDY, READ PAGES 215–224 OF *The Journey.*

- Read the sidebar on pages 94–95 of the Study Guide, and be prepared to discuss the information in reference to the lesson.
- Read and respond to the entire lesson in the Study Guide. Make note of significant things the Lord teaches you as you study.
- Pray, asking God to reveal to you the truths related to this lesson that are applicable to the class members who will attend the small-group session.

LEADING THE SMALL GROUP

Introduction: Introduce the lesson by highlighting *Think About It* on pages 91–92 in the Study Guide. Write on the board the quote at the beginning of the lesson and the Scripture verse on page 91.

Rewind: Write on the board **Pain and Suffering.** Call for volunteers to suggest events or experiences that might be characterized as painful. List responses on the board. Discuss typical responses to painful experiences in our lives. List responses on the board. Call for a volunteer to read aloud James 4:14, then discuss how we should respond to anyone who claims to know the future.

Call for volunteers to suggest some areas of life through which pain and suffering might come. Some possible ideas are health, finances, career, family, relationships, and so forth. Call for volunteers to identify things we can count on 100 percent of the time. List responses on the board. If not included, add **God** to the list. Discuss reasons people might believe God can't be counted on. Point out that we often believe God to be undependable when He doesn't do what we want Him to do when we want Him to do it.

If you need more background on suffering, consult the sidebar for this lesson.

Rethink: Arrange the class in small groups or in pairs, and instruct them to use the activity in the Study Guide to identify how we should respond to pain and suffering. After a few moments, call for volunteers to list their responses. There are some biblical principles that should govern our responses to pain and suffering.

1. *Be on guard against pain's dangers.* Direct participants to use the activity in the Study Guide to identify their responses when they deal with pain. Briefly review each response, and call for volunteers to identify why they responded in such a way. Call for a volunteer to read aloud Psalm 31:10. Discuss situations in which you had the feelings expressed by the psalmist. Call for other volunteers to respond accordingly.

2. *Ask God to help you learn the lessons that the pain can teach.* Call for volunteers to identify painful experiences that have had long-lasting positive effects. Read aloud Psalm 145:8. Discuss how we can know the truth of this verse—that God is near.

Reflect: One of the most difficult emotions to handle is grief. Grief is a natural response to a tragic event. Grief can be the result of an unexpected or an expected event. Read aloud 1 Thessalonians 4:13 and discuss how a believer's grief differs from that of non-believers. Ask: *How should believers respond to their grief?*

1. **Don't be surprised by grief.** Read aloud John 11:32. Call for volunteers to identify some situations in which they have experienced grief. List responses on the board. Point out that most of the time, grief is associated with a personal loss. The loss can be the loss of a loved one, a relationship, a job, or a valued possession such as a home. Grief isn't limited to the loss of life. Therefore, we shouldn't be surprised when we experience grief.

2. **Turn your grief over to God**. If anyone knows what it is like to experience grief, God does. He lost His Son on a Roman cross and,

because Jesus embodied our sin, had to turn away from His Son. Read aloud Psalm 55:22 and identify the burdens that God can handle. Call for volunteers to identify reasons people might not turn their grief over to God. Then call for a volunteer to read aloud 2 Corinthians 1:3–4. Point out that God is fully capable and able to take our grief so that we see Him rather than our situations.

3. **Surround your grief with gratitude.** It's tough to be thankful for grief, but we can be thankful for the God who loves us enough to sustain us through the grief. Read aloud Ephesians 5:20 and identify the areas in which we are to give thanks.

4. **Reach out to someone who also is hurting.** The situations you face uniquely qualify you to minister to others in their times of need. When you are experiencing grief, you can be certain that God is preparing you to help someone else. Rather than turning inward, turn outward and offer encouragement to others. Read aloud Galatians 6:2, identifying the burdens we are to be carrying.

React: Read aloud 1 Corinthians 13:12. Ask: *How did Paul deal with life's experiences?* Read Romans 8:38–39. Ask: *What is able to separate us from God?* Work through the React section of the Study Guide as you bring the lesson to a close.

Call attention to the "Three Truths" activity at the end of the lesson. Be prepared to share your three truths as an example. Close in prayer.

CONFRONTING THE ENEMIES WITHIN

CHAPTER ONE

WHAT WENT WRONG?

PREPARE TO LEAD

TO GET THE MOST FROM THIS STUDY, READ THE PREFACE AND pages 32–38 of *The Journey.*

- Read the sidebar on pages 5–6 of the Study Guide, and be prepared to discuss the information in reference to the lesson.
- Read and respond to the entire lesson in the Study Guide. Make note of significant things the Lord teaches you as you study.
- Pray, asking God to reveal to you the truths related to this lesson that are applicable to the class members who will attend the small-group session.

LEADING THE SMALL GROUP

Introduction: Introduce the lesson by highlighting *Think About It* on pages 3–4 in the Study Guide. Write on the board the quote at the beginning of the lesson and the Scripture verse on page 3.

Rewind: Write **Problems** on the board, and call for volunteers to identify some categories of problems they face. List responses on the board. Ask volunteers to suggest what might be God's role in solving some of the problems listed. Call for a volunteer to read aloud 2 Thessalonians 2:7, then direct participants to use the activity in the Study Guide to identify how the Bible characterizes evil. Point out that evil is a mystery and, therefore, we are unable to understand it. The sidebar deals more specifically with the concept of mystery as applied to God. For additional points of discussion, review the information in the sidebar on pages 5–6.

Rethink: Write on the board: **Good is . . .** Then call for volunteers to complete the statement. List responses on the board. In the Study Guide, there is an extensive explanation of "good" as being related to God as the standard. Ask participants to reflect on how good is determined in today's culture. Direct participants to use the activity in the Study Guide to identify the things that we consider good that were part of the original creation. The lesson is that we value things today that were never a part of God's initial declaration of "good." As a result, our definition of *good* is based on a standard much lower than God's original definition.

Write on the board: **The good life is . . .** Then call for volunteers to describe what they consider to be the good life. List responses on the board. Review the responses, highlighting that the real good life consists of those things that draw us closer to God.

Reflect: The Bible describes the relationship between God and humanity as originally being friendly. Ask if it is possible for people to be God's friends today. Call for those offering opinions to explain their rationale for their beliefs. Direct participants to use the Study Guide to identify their concepts of obedience. After a few minutes, review the possible responses in the Study Guide and point to examples of determining obedience in each way.

Call for participants to recount the story of Adam and Eve, citing the presence of free will in their lives. From their story, we can learn a lot about the process of determining right and wrong.

1. **They made a choice to love God.** Read aloud Genesis 2:25. Call for volunteers to describe the situation in which they first loved God. Then discuss what happens to that initial excitement. Ask: *Why is it that new believers often are more excited about their faith than are more seasoned believers?* Discuss responses.

2. **They made a choice to reject God**. Read aloud Genesis 3:1–6. The first mistake made by Adam and Eve was to willfully choose to do exactly what God said not to do. Call for volunteers to suggest some things that we do that we know are prohibited by God. List responses on the board. Direct participants to use the Study Guide to identify things Satan uses to distract believers from their relationships with God. Call for volunteers to share their responses. Call for volunteers

to read aloud Luke 10:18 and Isaiah 14:12–14 and to identify what each passage says about Satan.

Arrange the class in five small groups, and assign each group one of the following passages: Revelation 12:9–10; John 8:44; 1 Thessalonians 3:5; 1 John 3:12; and 1 Peter 5:8. Direct the groups to review the passages and to determine what each says about Satan and his work. After all groups have reported, ask volunteers to report how they have experienced Satan using these strategies against them.

Use the activity in the Study Guide to identify the specific sins of the serpent, Eve, and Adam. Discuss ways in which we fall into the same patterns of sin. Read aloud Romans 5:12, calling attention to the universal effect of the original sin.

React: Draw a connection between the sin in our lives and our closeness to God. Point out that we cannot be close to God when we have sin in our lives. Use the material under the React section of the Study Guide to bring the lesson to a close.

Call attention to the "Three Truths" activity at the end of the lesson. Be prepared to share your three truths as an example. Close in prayer.

CONFRONTING THE ENEMIES WITHIN

CHAPTER TWO

SIN'S DEVASTATION

PREPARE TO LEAD

TO GET THE MOST FROM THIS STUDY, READ PAGES 38–42 OF *The Journey.*

- Read the sidebar on page 26 of the Study Guide, and be prepared to discuss the information in reference to the lesson.
- Read and respond to the entire lesson in the Study Guide. Make note of significant things the Lord teaches you as you study.
- Pray, asking God to reveal to you the truths related to this lesson that are applicable to the class members who will attend the small-group session.

LEADING THE SMALL GROUP

Introduction: Introduce the lesson by highlighting *Think About It* on pages 23–24 in the Study Guide. Write on the board the quote at the beginning of the lesson and the Scripture verse on page 23.

Rewind: As participants arrive, direct them to use the activity in the Study Guide to identify their most common sins. After a few moments, call for volunteers to suggest the ultimate consequences of sin. Point out that the Bible doesn't teach that a life free from sin is possible; however, it does teach that the Christian life should be free from the control of habitual sin. Call for a volunteer to read aloud Romans 6:23. Discuss the concept of wages due for work done. Relate the concept to sin and the fact that there is a payment due for sin—death.

The sidebar for this lesson deals with gardens in the Bible. This is supplemental information for this lesson, or it can be used as an additional lesson at some point in the future.

Rethink: Ask participants to use the activity in the Study Guide to reflect on the timing for their realization of the consequences of their sin. Call for volunteers to signify by raising their hands which response best describes when they consider sin's consequences.

Sin has immediate and permanent consequences. Use the story of Adam and Eve as a backdrop for discussing the following points regarding the consequences of sin.

1. **Death entered the world.** In spite of God's desire that we live forever in perfect harmony with Him, Adam and Eve sinned and introduced death into our world. They were paid for their sin. The wage they received was death. There was no way for them to go back and un-sin. Call for a volunteer to read aloud Hebrews 9:27. Then call for volunteers to suggest what they expect to happen at judgment. Point out that death and judgment are inevitable; therefore, we must all be prepared to face God.

2. **We became separated from God.** Adam and Eve's sin resulted in them being afraid of God. Call for volunteers to suggest reasons people are afraid of God. List responses on the board. Being afraid of God is a sign of a ruptured relationship with God. Read aloud Isaiah 59:2 and point out that sin separates us from God.

3. **We became alienated from each other.** Prior to their fall, the relationship between Adam and Eve was smooth. However, once they sinned, they began to blame each other. Their relationship was permanently damaged.

4. **We became subject to God's judgment.** Call for a volunteer to read aloud Psalm 7:11, and discuss the kind of judge God is. Because of His character, God is just and within His rights to distance Himself from those who are rebellious.

5. **We became slaves of sin.** Call for a volunteer to read aloud Romans 7:21–23. Whereas Adam and Eve had the choice to rebel against

God, for us it is natural. We are sinful by nature and cannot, under our own power, keep from sinning.

6. **The whole creation was corrupted.** Read aloud Genesis 3:17–18 and discuss the universal effect of the original sin. Then read aloud Romans 8:21 and explain that things will return to the way God intended them to be when God's kingdom is reestablished following Christ's return.

Reflect: Direct participants to use the activity in the Study Guide to identify those specific sins in which they have been parties. Call for a volunteer to read aloud James 3:6, and call attention to the danger associated with a person's words. Direct participants to use the activity in the Study Guide to rate the characteristics of their thought lives, identifying those areas that are of significant concern to them. As time allows, use the information in the Study Guide to continue discussing this subject.

React: Call for participants to identify some things they have done to try to improve their lives. Ask them to reflect on the success of their efforts. Discuss the reasons people choose to pursue life change without pursuing a relationship with God. Point out that God has a plan for every person and that our greatest peace and satisfaction will come as a result of doing what God has designed us to do. Direct participants to use the Study Guide to draw the study of this lesson to a close.

Call attention to the "Three Truths" activity at the end of the lesson. Be prepared to share your three truths as an example. Close in prayer.

CONFRONTING THE ENEMIES WITHIN

CHAPTER THREE

PRONE TO WANDER

PREPARE TO LEAD

To get the most from this study, read pages 155–160 of *The Journey.*

- Read the sidebar on pages 46–47 of the Study Guide, and be prepared to discuss the information in reference to the lesson.
- Read and respond to the entire lesson in the Study Guide. Make note of significant things the Lord teaches you as you study.
- Pray, asking God to reveal to you the truths related to this lesson that are applicable to the class members who will attend the small-group session.

LEADING THE SMALL GROUP

Introduction: Introduce the lesson by highlighting *Think About It* on pages 43–44 in the Study Guide. Write on the board the quote at the beginning of the lesson and the Scripture verse on pages 43–44.

Rewind: Write **Stress** on the board, and call for volunteers to suggest some common sources of stress. List responses on the board. Discuss how people respond to stress. Ask: *At what point do people turn to God to deal with their stress?* Discuss responses. Point out that stress is the result of our reacting to the things that take place around us and, because we are so aware of world events, we are subject to more and more stress.

The sidebar for today's lesson relates to temptation and how it is realized in our lives. This can be used as supplemental information for today's lesson or as a lesson in its own right at some point in the future.

Rethink: Ask participants to identify the Scriptures they use to combat the temptations they face. List the Scriptures on the board. Be prepared to list some Scriptures you have identified prior to the class session. Read aloud Romans 8:26 and discuss the role of the Holy Spirit in our dealing with temptation. Temptation is universal and, therefore, we must have a plan for dealing with it. Arrange the class in small groups or pairs, and instruct them to use the activity in the Study Guide to identify how they might deal with each situation listed. After a few minutes, call for responses. Ask participants to identify the situation for which they are most prepared. Ask: *Why don't we prepare to face temptation?* Call for responses.

Reflect: Define *temptation* by writing on the board: **Being urged or enticed to do something wrong.** Use the list in the Study Guide to identify common sources of temptation. Point out that temptation often comes from everyday activities that we don't see as dangerous. Call for volunteers to read aloud Matthew 4:4, 7, and 10. Point out the common phrase in each of these verses. Read aloud 1 Peter 5:8, and call for volunteers to identify the universal source for all temptation. Ask volunteers to suggest what this verse says about Satan's purpose. Write that purpose on the board.

Read aloud 2 Corinthians 11:14, directing attention to Satan's mode of operation. Ask for volunteers to identify how they have seen this mode of operation at work in their lives. There are two ways that Satan works against us. It is important for us to guard ourselves against both avenues of attack.

1. **Satan pressures us from the outside.** Ask volunteers to identify some external sources of temptation that they see at work in their lives. List responses on the board. Arrange the class in small groups, and invite them to use the Study Guide to identify some common beliefs that are contrary to God's standards and how they respond to people who hold those opposing beliefs. After a few moments, call for responses. Read aloud 1 John 2:15–17 and highlight the phrase "ways of the world." Ask: *What are some common "ways of the world" that we deal with on a regular basis?* Call for responses.

2. **Satan pressures us from within ourselves**. Define "the flesh" as a determination to satisfy our personal desires and appetites to the exclusion of pleasing God. Discuss which pressure is greater—external

or internal. Call for those expressing opinions to defend their stances. Read aloud Romans 8:5, using the definition above in place of "the flesh." Call for volunteers to identify how they deal with internal pressures. Point out that we must all make the choice to live to pursue pleasing God rather than serving our own desires. What are some things we can do to make this a reality in our lives? Call for responses and list them on the board. Encourage participants to consider becoming a part of an accountability group to support their desire to fend off temptation and to please God.

React: Read aloud Romans 12:1, asking participants to identify the goal of the Christian life as defined by this verse. Read Romans 13:14, pointing out that there is a "dress code" for living the Christian life. Call for volunteers to suggest ways that they make this verse a reality in their lives. As appropriate, review the remainder of the React section to bring the lesson to a close. Read 1 Corinthians 10:32, making it a point to explain how serious it is to cause someone to stumble. Call for volunteers to suggest some ways we cause others to stumble. Point out that the Christian's freedom ends when the expression of that freedom interferes with someone's ability to see God for who He really is.

Call attention to the "Three Truths" activity at the end of the lesson. Be prepared to share your three truths as an example. Close in prayer.

CONFRONTING THE ENEMIES WITHIN

CHAPTER FOUR

THE WAY OF ESCAPE

PREPARE TO LEAD

TO GET THE MOST FROM THIS STUDY, READ PAGES 160–164 OF *The Journey.*

- Read the sidebar on pages 63–65 of the Study Guide, and be prepared to discuss the information in reference to the lesson.
- Read and respond to the entire lesson in the Study Guide. Make note of significant things the Lord teaches you as you study.
- Pray, asking God to reveal to you the truths related to this lesson that are applicable to the class members who will attend the small-group session.

LEADING THE SMALL GROUP

Introduction: Introduce the lesson by highlighting *Think About It* on pages 61–62 in the Study Guide. Write on the board the quote at the beginning of the lesson and the Scripture verse on page 61.

Rewind: Sin results in a variety of responses from the person who sinned. Direct participants to use the activity in the Study Guide to describe their responses when they realize they have sinned. After a few moments, call for volunteers to read their responses. Instruct participants to work together in small groups or pairs to develop a strategy for defeating temptation. Call for reports from each group.

One of the best personifications of problems is the story of David and Goliath. Goliath—the Philistine champion—seemed to love harassing the Israelites in the same way that problems taunt us. The sidebar in this lesson deals with this story. It can be used to supplement this lesson or as a separate lesson to be used later.

Rethink: Ask volunteers to identify situations for which they have emergency plans. List responses on the board. Ask participants to identify their rationale for having these plans. Call for volunteers to identify the spiritual evacuation plans they use in response to the temptations they face. Ask: *Why don't people have plans for evacuating in the event of a spiritual attack?* Call for responses.

Reflect: Dealing with temptation is something that requires a strategy. This lesson highlights four steps to dealing with temptation.

1. **Recognize temptation.** Ask participants to identify how they can recognize temptation in advance. List responses on the board. Point out that the only way to recognize temptation in advance is to have a thorough knowledge of God's standards. Ask: *Why is it so tough to identify right and wrong?* Direct participants to use the activity in the Study Guide to respond to this question. Call attention to the questions to ask yourself before taking part in any area about which you might be unsure. As you read the list of questions, remind the class that glorifying God is the Christian's primary responsibility.

2. **When temptation comes, reject it.** The longer you spend with temptation, the more comfortable you will be with it. Temptation is like a deadly poison—when you encounter it, take every precaution to make sure it doesn't affect you. Call for volunteers to read aloud 2 Timothy 2:22; 1 Corinthians 10:14; and 1 Corinthians 6:18. Summarize the advice each Scripture offers in regard to sin. Read aloud 1 Corinthians 10:13, and encourage the class to commit it to memory.

3. **Learn from your encounters with temptation.** Direct participants to use the activity in the Study Guide to list the people and situations that are most tempting to them. Encourage them to make defending themselves against these attacks a priority. Point out that we all have personal weaknesses that Satan targets for exploitation. If we know our weaknesses, we will be better prepared for Satan's attacks.

4. **When you fail, repent and seek God's forgiveness.** We all fail and disappoint God and ourselves. When we fail, it is the job of the Holy

Spirit to convict us of our sin. Ask participants to use the Study Guide to record the effect of sin on their personal relationships with God. Read aloud 1 John 1:9, and remind everyone that God's love leaves us with the assurance that we can be restored to a right relationship with God. However, mention the fact that some consequences of our sin persist even though we've been forgiven for the sin.

React: For Christians, sin not only damages their relationships with God, but it damages their reputations with unbelievers. It is important that we guard our lives so that we can make a difference in the lives of those who do not know God. Ask participants to identify their sources of hope. List responses on the board. Ask: *In what ways are we to be offering hope to a world that desperately seeks hope in things that come up empty?* Discuss responses.

Call attention to the "Three Truths" activity at the end of the lesson. Be prepared to share your three truths as an example. Close in prayer.

CONFRONTING THE ENEMIES WITHIN

CHAPTER FIVE

WHY DID IT HAPPEN?

PREPARE TO LEAD

TO GET THE MOST FROM THIS STUDY, READ PAGES 165–168 OF *The Journey.*

- Read the sidebar on pages 79–80 of the Study Guide, and be prepared to discuss the information in reference to the lesson.
- Read and respond to the entire lesson in the Study Guide. Make note of significant things the Lord teaches you as you study.
- Pray, asking God to reveal to you the truths related to this lesson that are applicable to the class members who will attend the small-group session.

LEADING THE SMALL GROUP

Introduction: Introduce the lesson by highlighting *Think About It* on pages 77–78 in the Study Guide. Write on the board the quote at the beginning of the lesson and the Scripture verse on page 77.

Rewind: Begin the session by discussing the concept of spiritual strength. Direct participants to use the activity in the Study Guide to rate their spiritual strength. Ask for volunteers to identify how they are strengthened spiritually. List responses on the board. Ask: *Is your spirituality insurance against hell or a way of life? How does your response to this question affect your view of spiritual matters?* Call for responses. Use the sidebar on the heart as supplemental information for this study. Keep in mind that the Bible uses the heart to represent the very center of a person's thinking.

Rethink: Direct participants to use the activity in the Study Guide to evaluate the condition of their spiritual hearts. After a few moments, instruct them to determine if a spiritual change of heart is possible in their lives and to record their responses in the space provided in the Study Guide. Write on the board the following quote from the Study Guide: **"We can't become the people God wants us to be by remaining the people we used to be."** Call for volunteers to react to this statement.

Reflect: Discuss the connection between a person's thinking and acting. Point out that actions follow thoughts, therefore long-term change must focus on a change in the way a person thinks. Write on the board **Rules** and **Principles**. Ask volunteers to suggest the differences between the two terms. Point out that rules can be circumvented, but principles are transferable from situation to situation.

Write on the board, **God's will for my life is . . .** Call for volunteers to read aloud 1 Thessalonians 4:3; 2 Corinthians 7:1; and Matthew 23:27. After each passage is read, list on the board how that verse completes the statement regarding God's will. In Matthew 23:27, the focus is on inner change. Why is a change of heart so important?

1. **Our thoughts determine our actions.** Any action is preceded by a mental spark, even if it is only a brief spark. Therefore, controlling our thoughts is central to changing our way of life. Call for a volunteer to read aloud Matthew 15:19. Ask: *According to this passage, what is inside a person's heart?*

2. **God loves us and knows how destructive wrong thoughts and emotions can be.** Describe a time when you did something you shouldn't have because you had bad thoughts or emotions. There is a connection between a person's emotional health and his or her physical health. Part of controlling our minds is controlling our emotions. Call for a volunteer to read aloud Psalm 32:3–4. Point out the results of David's attempt to hide his sin. Read aloud Proverbs 17:22. Discuss the differences between a cheerful spirit and a crushed spirit. Ask: *Which one is more pleasing to God? Why?* Direct participants to use the activity in the Study Guide to reflect on a time when they suffered physically because they had sin with which they had not yet dealt. However, point out that in the Study Guide, there is a statement that reminds us not to connect every physical ailment to sin. That way of thinking is faulty. Review this material so that you will be prepared to answer questions that follow this line of thinking. Read

aloud Colossians 1:21–22 and review a person's spiritual condition before salvation. Discuss how things change once a person accepts God's offer of eternal life.

React: The desire to be perfect seems to affect people of all types; the desire to be perfect before God, however, garners much less attention. Ask: *Why do people seek perfection but not perfection before God?* List responses on the board. Direct participants to follow along in the Study Guide as you bring the lesson to a close using the React section of this lesson. Based on the needs of your class, offer additional insights if needed.

Call attention to the "Three Truths" activity at the end of the lesson. Be prepared to share your three truths as an example. Close in prayer.

CONFRONTING THE ENEMIES WITHIN

CHAPTER SIX

THE ENEMIES WITHIN

PREPARE TO LEAD

To get the most from this study, read pages 169–174 of *The Journey.*

- Read the sidebar on pages 95–97 of the Study Guide, and be prepared to discuss the information in reference to the lesson.
- Read and respond to the entire lesson in the Study Guide. Make note of significant things the Lord teaches you as you study.
- Pray, asking God to reveal to you the truths related to this lesson that are applicable to the class members who will attend the small-group session.

LEADING THE SMALL GROUP

Introduction: Introduce the lesson by highlighting *Think About It* on pages 93–94 in the Study Guide. Write on the board the quote at the beginning of the lesson and the Scripture verse on page 93.

Rewind: As participants arrive, instruct them to use the activity in the Study Guide to rank themselves in the areas of pride, anger, envy, impurity, gluttony, slothfulness, and greed. Point out that these sins often are called the "seven deadly sins" based on the way they are discussed in Scripture. Work through the list, pointing to the acceptance and celebration of each sin in today's society. Discuss how these sins affect the day-to-day lives of well-meaning Christians. Focus on pride as you read aloud Proverbs 16:18. This verse describes the end result of pride, which was the sin of Satan before his expulsion from heaven. The sidebar focuses on the concept of hate as used in Scripture. Some people might struggle with the Bible's description of God as hating certain sins. Be sure to point out that God does hate sin, but He loves the sinner.

Rethink: Pride is a universal problem. Encourage participants to use the Study Guide to identify how they have been affected by personal pride. Call for volunteers to suggest ways to control personal pride. Read aloud Isaiah 14:13–14 and identify the primary problem described in this passage. The primary human problem has been the desire to be like God, and today the problem is bigger than ever. Call for a volunteer to read aloud Proverbs 16:18, and then identify the ultimate danger associated with pride.

Reflect: Pride has three direct effects in a person's life. Briefly describe each effect using the information provided and the additional information in the Study Guide.

1. **Pride blinds us to our faults.** Bring prideful prevents us from seeing ourselves the way we are. Read aloud Luke 18:11 and 13, calling attention to the attitude expressed by each verse. Direct participants to use the activity in the Study Guide to identify the characteristics of which they are most critical. Point out that we often are more sensitive to the faults of other people who are very similar to personal characteristics we possess.

2. **Pride cuts us off from others.** When we are prideful, we damage any interpersonal relationships we have. Pride is at the heart of many social problems in our culture. Read aloud Revelation 5:9 and discuss the fact that we are not entitled to hate anyone for any reason.

3. **Pride cuts us off from God.** Read aloud 2 Chronicles 26:16, and discuss the problems that led to the downfall of King Uzziah. Ask: *How can we prevent this from becoming our problem?* Read aloud Micah 6:8 and identify the three attitudes that God requires of us—to do what's right, to love other people, and to live in obedience to God.

Envy and greed present a second problem for our society. Describe some contemporary examples of the effects of envy and greed on our culture. Here are a few examples of the effects of envy and greed:

Envy and greed are costly. Read aloud Acts 5:1–11, highlighting the effects of envy and greed on Ananias and Sapphira. Call for volunteers to identify the moral of the story. List responses on the board.

Envy and greed harm society. Read aloud James 4:1–2, and point out the progression of envy and greed described in this passage. Discuss some ways we can eliminate envy and greed from our daily lives. List responses on the board.

Envy and greed harm us personally. Read aloud 1 Timothy 6:10, and discuss the negative effects of loving money. List on the board the effects suggested by the class members.

React: Pride, envy, and greed are so common that many people don't see them as problems. Yet they affect us personally, socially, and spiritually. Use the information in the Study Guide to point out the four ways to avoid the dangers associated with pride, envy, and greed.

Admit your problem and ask God to forgive you. Read aloud 1 Peter 5:6 and discuss the information in the Study Guide.

Learn to walk in God's presence every day.

Ask God to help you learn the secret of true contentment. Read aloud 1 Thessalonians 5:18, and discuss how it can be a reality for us in our daily lives.

Learn to trust God in everything. Read Hebrews 13:5 and Philippians 4:11. Discuss how people can become more content in their daily lives.

Call attention to the "Three Truths" activity at the end of the lesson. Be prepared to share your three truths as an example. Close in prayer.

EMBRACING THE GOOD NEWS

CHAPTER ONE

A NEW BEGINNING

PREPARE TO LEAD

TO GET THE MOST FROM THIS STUDY, READ THE PREFACE AND pages 53–55 of *The Journey.*

- Read the sidebar on pages 5–6 of the Study Guide, and be prepared to discuss the information in reference to the lesson.
- Read and respond to the entire lesson in the Study Guide. Make note of significant things the Lord teaches you as you study.
- Pray, asking God to reveal to you the truths related to this lesson that are applicable to the class members who will attend the small-group session.

LEADING THE SMALL GROUP

Introduction: Introduce the lesson by highlighting *Think About It* on pages 3–4 in the Study Guide. Write on the board the quote at the beginning of the lesson and the Scripture verse on pages 3–4.

Rewind: Write **Change** on the board, and direct participants to use the activity in the Study Guide to identify the amount of change they have experienced since becoming a Christian. Point out that some people experience more significant change than do others. When God enters a person or a situation, things can't stay the way they were. Call for volunteers to share about some of the changes they have been through in their personal or spiritual lives. Use the information in the sidebar to include a brief discussion about the concept of hypocrisy and how it affected the early church and still affects us today.

Rethink: Arrange the class in small groups, and ask them to use the activity in the Study Guide to identify what they expect to happen when someone accepts Jesus Christ as Lord and Savior. After a few minutes, call for responses. Then ask them to determine if these changes have taken place in their lives. Ask: *Why do we expect other people to change yet we resist change in our own lives?* Call for responses.

Use the story of Saul's (Paul's) conversion as the backdrop for this lesson. Read aloud Acts 22:7, highlighting the fact that Saul's actions against Christians were offensive to Christians but ultimately were offensive to Jesus Christ. Ask: *Is our failure to share Christ with other people equally as offensive as Paul's persecution of them?* Not offering salvation to someone is wishing an eternity in hell upon him, and this is the ultimate in persecution.

Several things changed in Paul's life. Call for volunteers to share how they have been changed in the following areas: ambition, vocation, purpose, and awareness of the needs of others. Allow several people to share their thoughts.

Reflect: Conversion is one thing; maturing is another. Read aloud Acts 2:40–41, and discuss the rapid expansion of the infant church. As believers were genuinely changed by the power of God working in their lives, others were changed. It was a chain reaction that resulted in the salvation of thousands on one day. The early church had a plan to lead people to the Lord, then grow them in their faith. It wasn't accidental; it was a four-step process that we would be wise to incorporate into our mode of operation today.

1. **The new believers were trained in doctrine.** Call for volunteers to identify some of the foundational beliefs of your church and/or denomination. Don't be surprised if this is a short list. Before the class session, make sure you clarify the theological foundations of your church so that you don't misrepresent them in the discussion. Read aloud Acts 2:42. Explain the importance of knowing the foundational elements of one's faith and being able to separate eternal issues from matters of church practice. For example, point out that people don't go to hell because they don't practice the Lord's Supper the way your church does; they go to hell because they reject God's gift of salvation through Jesus Christ.

2. **The new believers were trained in fellowship.** Define *fellowship* as "sharing in the lives of other believers." *Fellowship* is not the first name of a large hall in the church or a name for a covered-dish meal. Real fellowship requires an investment of time in the lives of others.

Discuss reasons people don't invest time in the lives of other believers. List responses on the board. Call for volunteers to report some of the events that have happened in their lives that have served as preparation for ministry to others. Discuss some ways that believers can invest time in the lives of other believers. List ideas on the board.

3. **The new believers were trained in the breaking of bread.** This is most likely a reference to the sacrament of the Lord's Supper as described in 1 Corinthians 11. Call for a volunteer to read aloud 1 Corinthians 11:23–26, and identify in the passage the purpose of the Lord's Supper. List the purpose on the board. Direct participants to use the activity in the Study Guide to identify their thoughts as they partake in the Lord's Supper.

4. **The new believers were trained in the discipline of prayer.** Call for volunteers to share with the class the last thing that happened that drove them to a season of prayer. Review the activity in the Study Guide in which students are asked to identify the purpose of prayer. If there is considerable discussion related to this issue, consider using the six-lesson study on prayer that is a part of this series.

React: As you bring the lesson to a close, work step-by-step through the React section of the Study Guide. Call for volunteers to share their responses to the questions at the beginning of the React section. Ask participants to reflect on their spiritual growth and to spend time in prayer thanking God for those who have been instrumental in their growth.

Call attention to the "Three Truths" activity at the end of the lesson. Be prepared to share your three truths as an example. Close in prayer.

EMBRACING THE GOOD NEWS

CHAPTER TWO

IS ANYTHING DIFFERENT?

PREPARE TO LEAD

TO GET THE MOST FROM THIS STUDY, READ PAGES 55–56 OF *The Journey.*

- Read the sidebar on pages 23–25 of the Study Guide, and be prepared to discuss the information in reference to the lesson.
- Read and respond to the entire lesson in the Study Guide. Make note of significant things the Lord teaches you as you study.
- Pray, asking God to reveal to you the truths related to this lesson that are applicable to the class members who will attend the small-group session.

LEADING THE SMALL GROUP

Introduction: Introduce the lesson by highlighting *Think About It* on pages 21–22 in the Study Guide. Write on the board the quote at the beginning of the lesson and the Scripture verse on page 21.

Rewind: On the board, reproduce the spiritual life diagram that is in the Study Guide on page 22. As participants arrive, instruct them to use the activity to evaluate their spiritual lives over the past twelve months. After a few moments, call for volunteers to identify the events that accompanied their high points. List those events on the board. Point out that spiritual highs and lows are normal; the challenge is to know how to deal with each situation when it happens. The sidebar is a more thorough explanation of regeneration. You might choose to use this as additional information for the study or save it for use later.

Rethink: Call for volunteers to identify times when they doubted their faith or their relationship with God. Ask them to reflect on the situations that caused these feelings. Be prepared to share your own thoughts regarding your doubts. Brainstorm some ideas that might be helpful in responding to someone who questions his or her faith. List responses on the board. Write **Demands** on the board and call for volunteers to suggest some of the demands they have on their lives. List responses on the board. Ask them to reflect on the effects these demands have on their relationship with God. Discuss how easy it is to take our eyes off of God and concentrate on the situations we face.

Reflect: When God lives inside of us through His Holy Spirit, we can be certain that life will be different. There will be struggles between God's desires and our personal desires, and between the old man and the new man. Call for volunteers to identify areas of life that we try to control rather than giving control of them to God. List responses on the board. Point out that salvation changes people in at least three ways.

1. **A change of heart.** Read aloud Ezekiel 36:26, calling attention to the change that is described in this verse. Write **Heart** on the board. Arrange the class in small groups or in pairs, and instruct them to discuss how God changes their hearts. After a few minutes, call for volunteers to report the results of their discussions. List a brief summary of each response on the board.

2. **A change of vision.** Call for a volunteer to read aloud John 3:3. Discuss the change in vision revealed in this verse. Write **Kingdom of God** on the board, and call for volunteers to suggest what the term might mean. Point out that *Kingdom of God* can be viewed as "spiritual matters." Explain that conversion makes it possible for a person to perceive spiritual matters through the eyes of the Holy Spirit. Call for volunteers to identify times in which they are certain that their perceptions of a situation were influenced by the Holy Spirit. Point out that our ability to understand spiritual things is connected to our spiritual growth. If we aren't growing, we won't understand spiritual things.

3. **A change of purpose.** We all are good at wanting our way. No one has to teach us to be selfish. However, when God moves in, the control of our lives is transferred from self to God. This means that

our desire in life is to please Him, not ourselves. Call for a volunteer to read aloud 2 Corinthians 5:17 and to identify the effect of salvation on a person's life purpose. List the response on the board. Make two columns on the board labeled **Before** and **After**. Use the columns to lead a discussion of the life change that accompanies rebirth. Use the activity in the Study Guide to lead the class to consider the areas of their former lives that they are clinging to. Discuss the frustration that accompanies this type of dual living.

React: Direct the class to use the activity in the Study Guide to identify the reasons they might resist the changes associated with their faith. Call for volunteers to share stories about their resistance and the frustration they experienced as a result. Point out that spiritual growth and resisting spiritual change are mutually exclusive. You either have one or the other. Lead the class to consider ways to improve their spiritual lives through the ministries of your church.

Call attention to the "Three Truths" activity at the end of the lesson. Be prepared to share your three truths as an example. Close in prayer.

EMBRACING THE GOOD NEWS

CHAPTER THREE

A NEW RELATIONSHIP

PREPARE TO LEAD

TO GET THE MOST FROM THIS STUDY, READ PAGES 56–58 OF *The Journey.*

- Read the sidebar on pages 40–41 of the Study Guide, and be prepared to discuss the information in reference to the lesson.
- Read and respond to the entire lesson in the Study Guide. Make note of significant things the Lord teaches you as you study.
- Pray, asking God to reveal to you the truths related to this lesson that are applicable to the class members who will attend the small-group session.

LEADING THE SMALL GROUP

Introduction: Introduce the lesson by highlighting *Think About It* on pages 37–38 in the Study Guide. Write on the board the quote at the beginning of the lesson and the Scripture verse on pages 37–38.

Rewind: Write on the board **Characteristics of Good Relationships**. As participants arrive, invite them to add to the list characteristics they believe to be crucial for good relationships. After a few moments, review the list and call for any additions. Then ask for volunteers to identify the characteristics of a good relationship with God. List responses in a separate column on the board. Discuss the differences between the two lists. Ask: *Is it easier to maintain a good relationship with a person or with God?* Call for volunteers to explain their responses.

The sidebar in this lesson deals with the concept of being an alien. An alien is a person who is living in a foreign culture. For that reason, believers often are referred to as aliens living on the earth. Use this material as supplemental to the discussion of relationships as it is needed.

Rethink: Arrange the class in small groups or in pairs, and instruct each group to work through the first three questions in the Rethink section of the Study Guide. Call for volunteers to suggest some of the benefits of the friendships they have with other believers. List responses on the board. Ask participants to explain why it is easier to share some things with friends than with God. Point out that God already knows whatever we are going to tell Him, so sharing with Him should be easier. Direct participants to use the activity in the Study Guide to describe their relationship with God. Ask them to identify the ideal relationship with God from the choices on the list. Discuss the reasons we aren't good friends with God. List responses on the board.

Reflect: Being God's friend doesn't mean that He overlooks our sins and our faults; it means that He has the right to confront us with anything He sees as being out of line with His purposes. Call for a volunteer to read aloud John 15:11–17. As you review the passage, point out these three points regarding friendship with God.

1. **Friendship with God is the source of real joy** (John 15:11). Call for volunteers to identify some of the things people do in order to pursue real joy. List responses on the board. Recount a time when you weren't experiencing godly joy, making sure to describe the quality of your relationship with God. Draw a horizontal line on the board. At the right end, write **Complaining** and at the left end write **Obeying**. Ask the class to consider where they are on the line. Point out that obedience requires us to put aside our personal wants.

2. **Friendship with God requires love** (John 15:12). Call for volunteers to identify situations in which it is difficult to love someone. List responses on the board. Brainstorm some ways to develop an attitude of love toward those who are difficult to love. List responses on the board. If anyone had a reason to not love people, it was Jesus. But because He was God, He lacked the capacity to do anything other than love people. When we fail to love people, we are failing to let the Holy Spirit work through us.

3. **Friendship with God requires obedience** (John 15:14). It is easy to do what God tells us to do as long as He tells us to do what we intended to do. Go back and read that statement again. Notice the conditional statement of Jesus: "You are my friends if . . ." Therefore, disobedience to God means that we are not His friends. Call for volunteers to suggest the conditions of their relationship with other people. List responses on the board. Then call for them to identify the conditions they must meet in order to be friends with certain people.

In addition to being God's friends, we are His children when we know Christ. Read aloud 1 Peter 1:23 and Ephesians 1:5, pointing out the birth and adoption aspects of our relationship with God. Being born into God's family and being adopted into God's family provides us a permanent relationship that can never be erased.

As time allows, direct the class to work together in small groups or in pairs to complete the remaining portion of the Reflect section of the Study Guide.

React: As you bring the class session to a close, direct participants to use the Study Guide to reconsider the truths of this lesson. Be sensitive to anyone in the class who might not be certain of his or her relationship with God. If the opportunity is there, speak with that person about his or her relationship with God.

Call attention to the "Three Truths" activity at the end of the lesson. Be prepared to share your three truths as an example. Close in prayer.

EMBRACING THE GOOD NEWS

CHAPTER FOUR

A NEW FAMILY

PREPARE TO LEAD

TO GET THE MOST FROM THIS STUDY, READ PAGES 58–59 OF *The Journey.*

- Read the sidebar on pages 55–56 of the Study Guide, and be prepared to discuss the information in reference to the lesson.
- Read and respond to the entire lesson in the Study Guide. Make note of significant things the Lord teaches you as you study.
- Pray, asking God to reveal to you the truths related to this lesson that are applicable to the class members who will attend the small-group session.

LEADING THE SMALL GROUP

Introduction: Introduce the lesson by highlighting *Think About It* on pages 53–54 in the Study Guide. Write on the board the quote at the beginning of the lesson and the Scripture verse on page 53.

Rewind: Write on the board **A New Family** and call for volunteers to suggest what it means to them to be the siblings of everyone else in the room. Be prepared for some humorous remarks. Ask the class to reflect on situations in which their spiritual family has been a source of strength and encouragement to them. Call for volunteers to share brief stories. Point out that our mobile society has made the spiritual family more important than ever. The sidebar provides additional information on the concept of the fellowship of believers. This information will be beneficial in the study of this lesson.

Rethink: Call for volunteers to list some television families. List responses on the board. Then lead a discussion about the concept of the perfect family. Identify and list on the board the characteristics of the perfect family. Then call for participants to determine if they would be invited to join the perfect family and to explain their reasons for their responses. Call for volunteers to suggest synonyms for *church* and list responses on the board. Direct them to complete the activity in the Study Guide in which they are asked to identify the biblical meaning of *church.*

In advance, gather basic information about the foundational beliefs of your church or denomination. If possible, gather the same information about a neighboring church. Rather than point out the differences, identify the similarities as you work through the Rethink section of the Study Guide.

Reflect: As part of God's family, we all have some privileges and responsibilities. We have the privilege of being in relationship with each other, and we have the responsibility to encourage and love one another. We have the privilege of traveling together on our faith journey, but we have the responsibility of forgiving one another when we come up short of God's standard. List additional privileges and responsibilities on the board. There are three facts to keep in mind about God's family.

1. **We realize the benefits of the family of God as we act in obedience to God.** Call for a volunteer to read aloud Matthew 12:48–50. Identify Jesus' two families—His family of origin and His family of disciples. According to Jesus' words, the spiritual ties are much stronger than the genetic ties. Call for class members to identify times when they had to choose between family and faith.

2. **As members of the family of God, we are heirs with Jesus Christ.** Call for class members to identify the benefits of being an heir. List responses on the board. Review the list of things God provides (in the Study Guide), and call for volunteers to discuss how they have experienced these nonmaterial blessings in their lives. Read aloud Romans 8:15–17 and identify the ultimate benefit associated with being an heir of God.

3. **As members of the family of God, all barriers are broken down.** Brainstorm some of the social barriers that have been a part of our

lifetimes. List responses on the board. Because God loves all people, He is able to accept people whom we reject. Only through His power can we overcome the barriers that we have held on to for years. Call for a volunteer to read aloud Ephesians 2:19–22. After hearing the passage, discuss what is included in the family of God. List responses in the space provided in the Study Guide. Then read through the possible responsibilities of being a child in God's family, and carefully consider how easy it is to fulfill each role identified in the Study Guide. Before ending this session, be sure to make it clear that everyone who believes that Jesus Christ is God's Son and that He is the only way to salvation is part of the same family—individual church practices are insignificant.

React: Direct class members to use the activity in the React section of the Study Guide to evaluate the time they spend maintaining their relationships with God as compared to the time they spend on things that are personal in nature. Discuss the meaning of this activity by pointing out how easy it is to focus on ourselves while leaving out God. List on the board some ideas that might be helpful in a person's desire to maintain his or her relationship with God.

Call attention to the "Three Truths" activity at the end of the lesson. Be prepared to share your three truths as an example. Close in prayer.

EMBRACING THE GOOD NEWS

CHAPTER FIVE

A NEW PURPOSE

PREPARE TO LEAD

TO GET THE MOST FROM THIS STUDY, READ PAGES 59–61 OF *The Journey.*

- Read the sidebar on pages 72–74 of the Study Guide, and be prepared to discuss the information in reference to the lesson.
- Read and respond to the entire lesson in the Study Guide. Make note of significant things the Lord teaches you as you study.
- Pray, asking God to reveal to you the truths related to this lesson that are applicable to the class members who will attend the small-group session.

LEADING THE SMALL GROUP

Introduction: Introduce the lesson by highlighting *Think About It* on pages 69–70 in the Study Guide. Write on the board the quote at the beginning of the lesson and the Scripture verse on pages 69–70.

Rewind: Draw a four-by-four chart on the board, and label the first column **My Purposes** and the second column **God's Purposes.** Then write in the four spaces in the first column the following words: *family, finances, faith,* and *future.* Repeat the words in the spaces in the second column. As class members arrive, instruct them to use the activity in the Study Guide to identify their purposes or goals in each area, then to identify God's purposes or goals for them in each area. After everyone has completed the activity, discuss the differences between our purposes and God's purposes. Ask class members to identify which category was the easiest to complete. Call for explanations of responses.

Write on the board **Religion** and **Relationship.** Use the material in the Study Guide to lead the discussion about the differences between empty religion and a real relationship with Jesus Christ. Consider adding to the class session a discussion of the material in the sidebar about the Pharisees and their influence on the early developments of Christianity.

Rethink: Erase the board and write the following words: **Today, This Week, This Year,** and **The Next Five Years.** Lead a discussion of the goals that class members might have for each period listed on the board. Discuss how these goals are established and pursued. Direct class members to use the activity in the Study Guide to identify their motivation for achieving their goals.

Reflect: We can't invite God into our lives, give Him control, and keep the same goals as before our salvation. When we give God control, His goals must become our goals. Call for a volunteer to read aloud Ephesians 2:10 and to identify our basic purpose in life. Write the response on the board. To achieve this goal requires motivation. Call for a volunteer to read aloud 2 Corinthians 5:14–16 in order to locate the source of our motivation. List that response on the board. Call for volunteers to suggest how these truths should affect our everyday lives. Only as we live in the power of the Holy Spirit can we make a difference in our world. There are three things the Holy Spirit does in each of our lives.

1. **The Holy Spirit helps us discern truth.** Write **Truth** on the board, and call for volunteers to suggest the source of real truth. Read aloud John 16:13. Truth is only available as we listen to and obey the promptings of the Holy Spirit. Ask: *If we are going to recognize the Holy Spirit when He speaks, what should we be doing each day?* Point out the importance of spending time alone with God and listening to Him as He speaks to us through His Word. Remind class members that God will never instruct us to do something that is a violation of the Bible.

2. **The Holy Spirit guides our steps.** Direct class members to use the activity in the Study Guide to identify the role of the Holy Spirit in their decision-making processes. Call for a volunteer to read aloud Acts 10:17–23 and to identify how God ordered Peter's steps. First, Peter sought God's direction. Second, he was in tune with God's Spirit. Third, Peter was obedient to God's instructions. Write on the

board **Seek, Listen, Obey**, and discuss why this process presents such a problem for some believers.

3. **The Holy Spirit tells us where to serve.** Knowing what to do is part of the battle; knowing where to do it is the other part. Call for volunteers to identify how they determine where God wants them to go. Read aloud Acts 16:6–10, pointing out that Peter's ideas about where to serve differed from God's ideas about where to serve. Call for volunteers to identify situations when they have had similar experiences. Discuss some of the reasons people don't immediately do what God wants them to do.

React: Remind the class that God has a plan for the world that involves Him using us for His purposes. When we yield to His purposes, we find the greatest joy and satisfaction in life. Allow class members a few moments to use the space provided in the Study Guide to write a prayer asking God to reveal His plan for them. After several moments, call for volunteers to read aloud their prayers. Then, use the remainder of the material in the React section to bring closure to this lesson.

Call attention to the "Three Truths" activity at the end of the lesson. Be prepared to share your three truths as an example. Close in prayer.

EMBRACING THE GOOD NEWS

CHAPTER SIX

A NEW DESTINY

PREPARE TO LEAD

TO GET THE MOST FROM THIS STUDY, READ PAGES 61–62 OF *The Journey.*

- Read the sidebar on pages 89–90 of the Study Guide, and be prepared to discuss the information in reference to the lesson.
- Read and respond to the entire lesson in the Study Guide. Make note of significant things the Lord teaches you as you study.
- Pray, asking God to reveal to you the truths related to this lesson that are applicable to the class members who will attend the small-group session.

LEADING THE SMALL GROUP

Introduction: Introduce the lesson by highlighting *Think About It* on pages 87–88 in the Study Guide. Write on the board the quote at the beginning of the lesson and the Scripture verse on pages 87–88.

Rewind: Write on the board, **What is eternal life?** As class members arrive, instruct them to use the activity in the Study Guide to record their responses to the question. Call for volunteers to describe times when they were graded on a curve. Ask: *What is the benefit to being graded on the curve?* Discuss responses. Point out that grading on the curve lowers our focus from the standard. We no longer seek to live up to the standard; we simply seek to do as well as possible. Discuss this rationale in relation to the idea of entering heaven. Ask: *Why doesn't God grade on the curve?* Call for responses. Review the information in the sidebar, and be prepared to include it in your discussion of the concept of eternal life.

Rethink: Ask class members to identify what their childhood dreams were related to adulthood, their vocations, and relationships. Point out that childish optimism leads us to believe we can be anything we want to be. Now fast-forward to the end of life. Instruct participants to use the space provided in the Study Guide to list what they want to be their most significant contribution to the world. After a few moments, call for volunteers to read their responses aloud. Ask what steps they are taking to make this dream a reality. Use the activity in the Study Guide to identify some of the ways people are planning for their futures. Ask them to evaluate their responses and to circle any responses that are spiritual in nature. Discuss the significance of not having any spiritual aspirations.

Reflect: There are six evidences that your life has been affected by the presence of the Holy Spirit living inside you, and that you are seeking to walk with Christ every day.

1. **Renounce the world and its ways.** Read Galatians 5:19–21, and identify the characteristics that should or should not be a part of a believer's way of life. List responses on the board. Call for a volunteer to read aloud Luke 18:28–30 and identify those things that must be renounced in order to pursue a relationship with God.

2. **Commit your life to Christ.** Read aloud John 3:14–15, and list the steps necessary to receive eternal life. Write on the board *decision* and *commitment.* Call for volunteers to identify the differences between these two words. There are many people who make decisions without making a commitment to Jesus.

3. **Invest your life in service to God.** Call for class members to use the activity in the Study Guide to identify their attitudes toward service to God as being either a pleasure or a chore. Call for volunteers to suggest reasons that many Christians see their service to God as a chore. Read aloud John 4:35–36, and discuss the idea of participating in God's harvest.

4. **Sacrifice self for the benefit of the kingdom.** Write **Self** and **Others** on the board, and discuss which one our world suggests should be the focus of our lives. Read aloud John 12:25, and call for a volunteer to suggest how this verse compares to the modern way of thinking.

Point out that the battle for believers is between yielding to a desire to please self versus the desire to please God. Call for volunteers to suggest ways to keep God at the center of our lives. List suggestions on the board.

5. **Grow in your knowledge of God.** Read aloud John 17:3, and discuss some of the ways we can be more focused on growing in our knowledge of God. Be ready to identify some of the opportunities for growth provided through the ministries of your church.

6. **Plant seeds that produce spiritual fruit.** Read aloud Galatians 6:8 and identify some of the things people do to please their sinful natures. Direct participants to use the activity in the Study Guide to identify some ways they can avoid sowing to please the sinful nature and, instead, sow to please God. Call for class members to reflect on their lives and to determine which nature they are seeking to please more.

React: As you bring the class to a close, direct class members to quietly work through the activities in the React section of the Study Guide. Point out some specific ways we can better reflect God in our everyday lives.

Call attention to the "Three Truths" activity at the end of the lesson. Be prepared to share your three truths as an example. Close in prayer.

BUILDING A CHRIST-CENTERED HOME

CHAPTER ONE

ONE DAY AT A TIME

PREPARE TO LEAD

TO GET THE MOST FROM THIS STUDY, READ THE PREFACE AND pages 227–236 of *The Journey.*

- Read the sidebar on pages 5–6 of the Study Guide, and be prepared to discuss the information in reference to the lesson.
- Read and respond to the entire lesson in the Study Guide. Make note of significant things the Lord teaches you as you study.
- Pray, asking God to reveal to you the truths related to this lesson that are applicable to the class members who will attend the small-group session.

LEADING THE SMALL GROUP

Introduction: Introduce the lesson by highlighting *Think About It* on pages 3–4 in the Study Guide. Write on the board the quote at the beginning of the lesson and the Scripture verse on page 3.

Rewind: Call for volunteers to identify some of the kinds of problems they have faced in the previous twenty-four hours. Discuss the positive and negative spiritual effects of the problems we face. In the Christian life, we not only get to face our own problems, but also the problems of other believers with whom we have personal relationships. Refer to the sidebar on worldliness, and discuss how it affects believers in their pursuit of a relationship with God.

Rethink: Direct class members to work together in pairs or in small groups to discuss some situations in which their faith in God went cold. Encourage them to evaluate the situations so that they can determine some possible causes for their cold faith. Recount the story of Demas, then read aloud 2 Timothy 4:10. Ask class members to identify the source of Demas's downfall.

Ask class members to list some things they purchased but never used. List responses on the board. Discuss the reasons people don't use some of the items they purchase. Call for volunteers to identify their intentions when they established a personal relationship with Jesus Christ. List responses on the board. Then discuss how those intentions have been fulfilled or altered.

Reflect: Encourage participants to use the activity in the Study Guide to evaluate their total time commitment in the average day. It is normal for the total to exceed twenty-four hours because some activities occur simultaneously. Read aloud 2 Peter 3:18, and identify the command in this verse. Discuss the following biblical guidelines for time management.

1. **See each day as a gift from God.** Read aloud Psalm 31:15, and identify the attitude of the psalmist toward each day. Discuss some ways we can develop this attitude in our daily lives.

2. **Commit your time to God.** Read aloud Psalm 90:12, and discuss the end result of honoring God with our time. Discuss some ways in which we might see God's wisdom work in our daily lives.

3. **Set aside time for God and for others.** We must make spending time in godly pursuits a priority. We cannot maintain strong relationships with people or with God without investing time in doing so.

4. **Take time for your own needs.** Read aloud Mark 6:31, and call for volunteers to identify the places they go to be alone with God and to rest. Encourage class members to take this aspect of their spiritual lives very seriously.

One of the places in which believers often struggle is in their vocations. Work is ordained by God, but it isn't intended to be rigorous or intolerable. The following are some guidelines for allowing God to work through your vocation.

1. *View your work as a God-given responsibility.* Read aloud Ecclesiastes 2:24, and discuss what makes for satisfying work.

2. *Be faithful in your work.* Read aloud Colossians 3:22 and Colossians 4:1. Discuss the appropriate attitude of believers toward their work and an employer's attitude toward employees.

3. *Work with integrity.* If possible, bring some newspapers to class in which the stories of an employee's lack of integrity are reported. If you do not have access to the papers, be prepared to discuss some high-profile stories in which a lack of integrity was the root of the problem. As believers, it is important that we do nothing that might be misconstrued as inappropriate. If we do, we not only damage our lives, but also the reputation of our Lord. Read aloud Ephesians 5:8–11, and discuss how this passage relates to the idea of work.

React: Faith that is left unattended will be overwhelmed by the cares of the world. Call for class members to identify areas in which they are most likely to experience problems. List responses on the board. Point out that knowing that these areas are concerns should motivate us to strengthen ourselves against problems in these areas. Work through the remainder of the React section as you bring the session to a close.

Call attention to the "Three Truths" activity at the end of the lesson. Be prepared to share your three truths as an example. Close in prayer.

BUILDING A CHRIST-CENTERED HOME

CHAPTER TWO

FORKS IN THE ROAD

PREPARE TO LEAD

TO GET THE MOST FROM THIS STUDY, READ PAGES 237–246 OF *The Journey.*

- Read the sidebar on pages 23–24 of the Study Guide, and be prepared to discuss the information in reference to the lesson.
- Read and respond to the entire lesson in the Study Guide. Make note of significant things the Lord teaches you as you study.
- Pray, asking God to reveal to you the truths related to this lesson that are applicable to the class members who will attend the small-group session.

LEADING THE SMALL GROUP

Introduction: Introduce the lesson by highlighting *Think About It* on pages 21–22 in the Study Guide. Write on the board the quote at the beginning of the lesson and the Scripture verse on pages 21–22.

Rewind: Arrange the class in small groups or in pairs, and instruct them to discuss their perceptions of God's will for their lives. Call for each group or pair to report its ideas, and then call for volunteers to identify ways in which they are living out God's will in their daily lives. There is additional information in the sidebar related to the concept of God's will and how it is realized in the lives of believers.

Rethink: Keep the class arranged in small groups or in pairs, and invite them to complete the interactive activity in which they are asked to identify the aspects of life that are not a part of God's will. Ask: *How often do you ask God about His will for you?* Call for responses.

Write on the board **General Will** and **Individual Will**. Define the general will as God's will for all people and the individual will as God's specific will for each individual. Point out that the individual will always falls within the boundaries of the general will. The general will deals with morality and ethics. At no point are we exempt from living by God's standards. Call for volunteers to identify ways they can determine God's general will. The source, of course, is the Bible. Read aloud 2 Timothy 3:16, highlighting the functions of the Bible in the lives of believers. Write these functions on the board. Then read aloud Romans 13:7 and 1 Corinthians 6:18, calling attention to the specific instructions in these passages. Call for a volunteer to read aloud Luke 10:27 and to identify the principle in that verse.

God's individual will can be found in Jeremiah 29:11. Call for a volunteer to read aloud that verse, then discuss its implications in terms of God's individual will for His followers.

Reflect: One of the most puzzling aspects of the Christian life is the search for God's will. We can be certain that God is not playing hide-and-seek with His will. His will sometimes is obvious; we just don't see it because we don't want to do it, or we have allowed other things to get in the way. The Bible, however, does offer some advice for discovering God's will. Discuss these six things that can be done.

1. **Commit your decision to God.** Read aloud Psalm 86:11 and identify the teacher and the student. Discuss the fact that many believers expect God to conform to their desires rather than them conforming to His desires.

2. **Search the Scriptures.** If we know what the Scripture says, we can be sure that God's will falls within the boundaries. However, if we are ignorant about the scriptural guidelines, we can be certain we will be confused about God's will for our lives. Call for class members to identify Scriptures they consult when they are seeking God's will regarding a decision they are facing. List Scriptures on the board.

3. **Understand your circumstances.** God often uses circumstances to guide us, but we must be in tune to God's Spirit if we are going to

see Him work through our lives. Call for volunteers to describe times when God's will was revealed through their circumstances. Be careful not to over-spiritualize every event in life.

4. **Seek godly advice.** Ask class members to identify the people to whom they turn when they need spiritual advice. Read aloud Proverbs 15:22, identifying the people from whom God's people should seek advice.

5. **Trust the guidance of the Holy Spirit.** Read aloud Isaiah 30:21 and John 16:13. Discuss the role of the Holy Spirit in the everyday experiences of God's people. Call for volunteers to suggest reasons people don't listen to the Holy Spirit. List responses on the board.

6. **Trust God for the outcome.** Call for a volunteer to read aloud Proverbs 3:5–6. Discuss the instructions in this passage and the difficulty we have in obeying this passage. Read aloud the final phrase of the passage—*He will direct your paths.* If God isn't directing our paths, then we aren't trusting Him to do so.

React: Direct class members to identify those things that might be hindering them from understanding God's will in their lives. Review the general will, and challenge everyone in the class to seek to live within the boundaries of God's general will. In doing so, we will be conformed to His image, and we will discover God's individual will.

Call attention to the "Three Truths" activity at the end of the lesson. Be prepared to share your three truths as an example. Close in prayer.

BUILDING A CHRIST-CENTERED HOME

CHAPTER THREE

FOR BETTER OR FOR WORSE

PREPARE TO LEAD

To get the most from this study, read pages 247–251 of *The Journey.*

- Read the sidebar on pages 41–43 of the Study Guide, and be prepared to discuss the information in reference to the lesson.
- Read and respond to the entire lesson in the Study Guide. Make note of significant things the Lord teaches you as you study.
- Pray, asking God to reveal to you the truths related to this lesson that are applicable to the class members who will attend the small-group session.

LEADING THE SMALL GROUP

Introduction: Introduce the lesson by highlighting *Think About It* on pages 39–40 in the Study Guide. Write on the board the quote at the beginning of the lesson and the Scripture verse on page 39.

Rewind: Write **Marriage** on the board, and call for volunteers to offer definitions. Draw two lines from the word *marriage*. Label one line **Husband** and the other **Wife**. Call for volunteers to suggest the roles of the husband and wife within the marriage relationship. List responses on the board. Ask class members to determine if today's definitions of marriage are influenced more by the Bible or by cultural trends. Discuss responses. Read aloud Genesis 2:18, and identify God's purpose in creating the woman. Then read aloud Genesis 2:21–23, calling attention to the uniqueness of the creation of the woman. The sidebar for this lesson focuses on marriage. Review the information in the sidebar to determine if it is necessary for your discussion.

Rethink: Call for examples of the "perfect" marriage. Identify the characteristics that made it perfect. List them on the board. Ask class members to express their opinions as to whether or not it is possible to have a perfect marriage. Read aloud Genesis 2:18, and identify what God declared "not good." Discuss how this idea relates to the concept of marriage. Call for a volunteer to read aloud Genesis 2:24, and direct class members to respond to the activity in the Study Guide.

Reflect: At a time in our history when people debate the institution of marriage, it is important that we reintroduce ourselves to the biblical concept of marriage and discover just why God invented marriage in the first place.

1. **God gave us marriage for our companionship.** When God surveyed His creation, He could not find a companion for Adam. For that reason, He created Eve. The first marriage provided companionship. Ask students to reflect on the characteristics of God that were part of Adam. Because He was like God, Adam had the capacity to love and the desire to be loved. This capacity and desire still is a part of the human existence. Read aloud Genesis 2:20, highlighting the phrase "suitable helper." This phrase is a statement of purpose, not hierarchy. It is one thing to need a companion; it is another thing to be a companion. Call for volunteers to suggest characteristics of a good companion. List responses on the board. Selfishness can become a problem for marriage partners. Instruct class members to use the activity in the Study Guide to identify situations in which they have been selfish and to evaluate how being selfish affects their relationships with their spouses.

2. **God gave us marriage for our mutual help and encouragement.** We already have seen that Adam needed a suitable helper. Call for volunteers to suggest meanings for the word *suitable.* Point out that *suitable* means adequate, comparable, and similar. Describe how the concept of suitability will be beneficial in a marriage relationship.

3. **God gave us marriage for our mutual happiness and pleasure.** Marriage was never intended to be a chore; God intended it to be a pleasure. Read Genesis 2:23 and identify how Adam responded when Eve was created. God created Adam and Eve to be mutually pleasing to each other in every way. The boundaries for this pleasure, however,

were defined as marriage. Enjoying the pleasures of marriage outside of the marriage relationship is a violation of biblical principles. In addition to the physical benefit, the marriage relationship is an important arena for spiritual growth and encouragement. Read aloud Proverbs 6:27–29, and identify the consequences of living outside the boundaries defined by God. List responses on the board.

React: Depending on the makeup of your class, the application for this lesson will be different. If you are leading a class of people who have never been married, then the application will be future. If you are leading a class of married people, you will have to tailor the application to suit their stages in life—newly married to seasoned veterans to those who have been married more than once. Be careful to approach the application with a full awareness of the needs of the people in the class. Use the React section of the Study Guide to bring the lesson to a close.

Call attention to the "Three Truths" activity at the end of the lesson. Be prepared to share your three truths as an example. Close in prayer.

BUILDING A CHRIST-CENTERED HOME

CHAPTER FOUR

BEING A FAMILY

PREPARE TO LEAD

TO GET THE MOST FROM THIS STUDY, READ PAGES 251–256 OF *The Journey.*

- Read the sidebar on pages 57–59 of the Study Guide, and be prepared to discuss the information in reference to the lesson.
- Read and respond to the entire lesson in the Study Guide. Make note of significant things the Lord teaches you as you study.
- Pray, asking God to reveal to you the truths related to this lesson that are applicable to the class members who will attend the small-group session.

LEADING THE SMALL GROUP

Introduction: Introduce the lesson by highlighting *Think About It* on pages 55–56 in the Study Guide. Write on the board the quote at the beginning of the lesson and the Scripture verse on pages 55–56.

Rewind: Write **Family** on the board, and call for volunteers to offer adjectives to describe the family. List responses on the board. Call for volunteers to describe the greatest challenges facing the family. List responses on the board. Discuss the social concept of the family and how it has changed over the years. Call for examples of classic families, and discuss the roles of each person in the family. Describe the family as being the ideal setting for physical, emotional, and spiritual growth, yet in today's culture many parents have reassigned these tasks to other institutions—the school, athletic associations, and churches.

If appropriate for your class, discuss the concept of child abuse as presented in the sidebar on pages 57–59. This concept has biblical examples but might not be suited for every class setting.

Rethink: Explain that the spiritual training of individuals in the family is important. Direct class members to use the activity in the Study Guide to identify the person or institution that is responsible for the spiritual development of the members of the family. Then challenge them to grade themselves on their spiritual leadership in the home. Point out that many people don't value spiritual development as much as they value other aspects of life. Direct class members to use the activity in the Study Guide to evaluate their priorities. Then call for volunteers to suggest ways to make the spiritual growth of the family a higher priority.

Reflect: List on the board **Divorce**, **Abuse**, **Neglect**, **Poverty**, **Alcoholism**, **Violence**, and **Death**. Ask the class members to raise their hands if they have been affected in their family by at least one item on the list. Then call for raised hands by those who have been affected by more than one of the items on the list. Point out that everyone deals with family stresses that require them to search for answers and/or comfort. Read aloud Psalm 32:10, and call for volunteers to identify the people who fulfill this role in their lives. Ask them to report how many of the people listed are members of their families. It is God's wisdom that will unify the family so that the members can be beneficial to one another and supportive in times of need.

Read aloud Galatians 5:22–23, and direct participants to use the activity in the Study Guide to identify the characteristics that are their strongest. Discuss how these characteristics come into play within the family structure. Then call for participants to review the list and to identify the characteristics that are their weakest. Discuss how these characteristics negatively affect the family relationship.

Write on the board, **The spiritual health of a society depends on the spiritual health of its families.** Call for volunteers to react to the statement. Ask them to project their spiritual health onto the entire community and to evaluate the resulting spiritual health of the society. Satan's first attack pitted husband against wife and led to accusations and blame. Adam blamed Eve, and Eve blamed the serpent. Today, people still have problems taking responsibility for their actions.

Call for class members to use the activity in the Study Guide to identify the greatest source of strife in their relationships. Point out that each item on the list can be a significant source of problems within a family, so we must be careful in every area. Read aloud Matthew 6:24, and identify the two potential masters described in this verse. Point out that choosing to serve one means turning your back on the controlling power of the other. When we choose to serve money, we choose to prevent God from controlling our lives. When we choose to serve God, we choose to prevent money from controlling our lives. One of these decisions is good for the family; the other is bad for the family.

React: As you bring the lesson to a close, use the activities in the React section of the Study Guide to remind participants of the truths of this lesson. Point out that the ultimate goal for individuals is to please God and, in doing so, to please other people.

Call attention to the "Three Truths" activity at the end of the lesson. Be prepared to share your three truths as an example. Close in prayer.

BUILDING A CHRIST-CENTERED HOME

CHAPTER FIVE

BROKEN DREAMS

PREPARE TO LEAD

To get the most from this study, read pages 257–260 of *The Journey.*

- Read the sidebar on pages 74–75 of the Study Guide, and be prepared to discuss the information in reference to the lesson.
- Read and respond to the entire lesson in the Study Guide. Make note of significant things the Lord teaches you as you study.
- Pray, asking God to reveal to you the truths related to this lesson that are applicable to the class members who will attend the small-group session.

LEADING THE SMALL GROUP

Introduction: Introduce the lesson by highlighting *Think About It* on pages 71–72 in the Study Guide. Write on the board the quote at the beginning of the lesson and the Scripture verse on page 71.

Rewind: As class members arrive, direct them to use the activity in the Study Guide to identify all of the relationships they have had in which there was never a problem. Use the activity to point out that problems are a reality in just about every relationship. Ask participants to identify their initial responses when they have a problem. Call for volunteers to describe their reactions when they encounter interpersonal problems.

Ask class members to identify reasons that so many marriages resemble corporate mergers rather than the biblical ideal for marriage. Discuss what drives people to get married and why, in their opinion, so many marriages fail. List responses on the board. The sidebar for this lesson is on the topic of divorce and the biblical teachings on the subject. This is a controversial subject, so approach it with care, being sure not to condemn people who have been divorced. Divorce is a sin that has far-reaching effects, but other sins are equally harmful.

Rethink: As a group, complete the activity in the Study Guide in which the student is challenged to define divorce as being the norm . . . no one stays married now; a good thing for everyone involved; not God's perfect plan; or something to look forward to. Divorce is not the emergency parachute for a relationship gone bad. Discuss society's take on divorce by working through the second activity in the Rethink section of the Study Guide.

Reflect: Divorce has consequences for the divorcing couple and for a variety of other people closely connected to the couple. From children to friends, divorce alters relationships and the ways in which people interact. The fact is that divorce, like any other sin, is a failure to live up to God's standards. The good news is that God is in the business of restoration, and He has offered some guidelines for restoring a right relationship with Him following any failure in our lives. Be sure to point out that this process is applicable to every area of life. Before discussing the process, read aloud Matthew 7:24–29.

1. **Pay attention to what God says.** Reread Matthew 7:24 and identify the two actions Jesus requires of those who hear Him. Point out that "these sayings" refer to everything Jesus had said in the Sermon on the Mount. Call for volunteers to suggest situations in which we often are selective about doing what Jesus said. List responses on the board. The first step to restoration is agreeing with Jesus about what we did in the past. We must call sin what it is and admit to God that we let Him down. That means we must know God's standards as revealed in His Word.

2. **Expect the storms.** Reread Matthew 7:25 and call for participants to identify some of the things we do in preparation for a physical storm. List responses on the board. Then suggest that class members consider the storms they are facing in their lives. Ask: *As compared to our preparation for physical storms, how prepared are we for personal storms in life?* Call for responses. Discuss some of the things we can learn from the storms we face and how those experiences can serve to strengthen us spiritually. Direct class members to use the activity in

the Study Guide to identify their commitment to strengthening their spiritual foundations.

3. **Watch for weaknesses.** Reread Matthew 7:26–27 and identify the ultimate consequence of not obeying God's Word. List that consequence on the board. Point out that Satan often is more aware of our weaknesses than we are. For that reason, he will attack us at our most vulnerable point—which often is an area in which we have had a problem in the past. Arrange the class in small groups or pairs, and allow them time to develop a strategy for defending themselves against a repeat of past failures. After a few moments, call for groups to report their findings. List responses on the board, creating an agreed-upon strategy for overcoming personal weaknesses.

React: Read aloud Matthew 7:28–29, and point out that the ultimate goal in life is for people to be astonished at what God does, not what we do. Through our weaknesses, God can work to restore us to a right relationship with Him and, in the process, be glorified in and through our lives. Direct class members to work through the activities in the React section of the Study Guide. Then, as time permits, enter a season of prayer in which you allow the class members to voice their concerns to God.

Call attention to the "Three Truths" activity at the end of the lesson. Be prepared to share your three truths as an example. Close in prayer.

BUILDING A CHRIST-CENTERED HOME

CHAPTER SIX

PREVENTIVE MEDICINE

PREPARE TO LEAD

To get the most from this study, read pages 260–266 of *The Journey.*

- Read the sidebar on pages 89–91 of the Study Guide, and be prepared to discuss the information in reference to the lesson.
- Read and respond to the entire lesson in the Study Guide. Make note of significant things the Lord teaches you as you study.
- Pray, asking God to reveal to you the truths related to this lesson that are applicable to the class members who will attend the small-group session.

LEADING THE SMALL GROUP

Introduction: Introduce the lesson by highlighting *Think About It* on pages 87–88 in the Study Guide. Write on the board the quote at the beginning of the lesson and the Scripture verse on pages 87–88.

Rewind: As class members arrive, call for them to use the activity in the Study Guide to identify some of the things they do on a regular basis to strengthen their spiritual lives. After a few moments, call for volunteers to report their thoughts. List responses on the board. Discuss the activities listed and offer any additional activities that might be beneficial. Point out that being strengthened spiritually is the same as being immunized against a disease—you don't realize you need it until it's too late. Write on the board the slogan, **Only you can prevent forest fires.** Inform the class that the slogan used by Smokey Bear taught a generation that prevention requires forethought. When it comes to our families and our marriages, the same degree of forethought will protect us against the dangers of divorce. The sidebar on social structures in biblical times will be of value in some situations. You might use the information as supplemental to this lesson or for future lessons.

Rethink: Direct attention to the activities in the Study Guide, and call for participants to suggest the most important parts of the marriage relationship. List responses on the board. Then call for volunteers to identify the sources for their thoughts. List responses on the board. Relate the story of the leak in the dam as it appears in the Study Guide, then call for volunteers to suggest some things that will strengthen marriages and interpersonal relationships. List responses on the board. Ask: *Why don't people do these things?* Call for responses.

Reflect: At a time when more than 50 percent of all marriages end in divorce, it is important to review the biblical advice regarding the issue of marriage. Some researchers have reported that the rate of divorce among Christians actually is higher than the rate of divorce among the general public. Whereas the tendency is to evaluate what happened, the real solution is to engage in some preventive maintenance. Here are three things you can do to keep the flame alive.

1. **Commit your marriage relationship to God.** Marriage was God's idea, so it stands to reason that the best solution for keeping the marriage running properly is to keep it closely connected to the Master Mechanic. Call for volunteers to suggest some of the places people turn when their marriages get tough. List responses on the board. Discuss the rationale for turning to these sources of help rather than turning to God. Write on the board: **A good marriage is a 50-50 relationship**. Call for class members to react to the statement before pointing out that marriage requires 100 percent of the effort from everyone involved. Refer to the Study Guide, and call for class members to identify what it means to commit your marriage to God. Point out that a marriage commitment is a daily commitment to God's best. Call for a volunteer to read aloud Exodus 20:14, and identify the specific command in this verse. Call for a volunteer to read aloud Proverbs 6:32, and discuss the specific dangers associated with adultery. Encourage class members to use the space provided in the Study Guide to list their plan of action when the opportunity to commit adultery comes along. Point out that this is their spiritual life raft, intended to carry them from danger to safety.

2. **Commit yourself to your marriage.** Call for volunteers to identify some of the things that demand their attention during the day. List responses on the board. Be sure to include work, hobbies, children, socializing, household chores, and so forth. Point out that it is easy for the things on the list to slowly creep up the list of priorities and to overtake marriage. Call for volunteers to suggest some warning signs that a marriage might be in trouble. List responses on the board. Read aloud Ephesians 5:25. Call for volunteers to identify the specific instruction in this verse. Write that instruction on the board. Then direct class members to use the activity in the Study Guide to identify how their routine activities affect their marriages. Point out that it is easy to get so focused on ourselves that we ignore God's instruction to maintain our marriages.

3. **Treat each other with affection and respect.** Some marriages are characterized by mutual affection that is obvious to the most casual observer. Others, however, are much more volatile in nature. It is natural for people to seek affection and respect. If that doesn't come through the marriage relationship, it will be sought in other ways. Read aloud Ephesians 5:33 and 1 Peter 3:7. What do these passages say about the roles within the marriage relationship? Direct attention to the activity in the Study Guide that calls for marriage partners to evaluate their communication with their spouses. Direct class members to complete the activity. Read aloud Hebrews 3:13, and discuss some practical ways spouses can encourage one another. List responses on the board. Read aloud 1 Timothy 5:22, and discuss

some ways to protect the purity of the marriage relationship and the home. List ideas on the board.

React: Use the React section of the Study Guide to bring the lesson to a close. If appropriate, allow time for spouses to write notes of commitment to each other, and give them time to share their notes with each other. If there are no married couples in the class, call for the class to write notes of commitment to their future spouses or to God. Read aloud 1 Peter 3:3–4, and discuss the dangers of pursuing outer beauty rather then inner beauty. Discuss some ways to make pursuing inner beauty a priority for both men and women.

Call attention to the "Three Truths" activity at the end of the lesson. Be prepared to share your three truths as an example. Close in prayer.

LEARNING TO PRAY

CHAPTER ONE

THE PRIVILEGE OF PRAYER

PREPARE TO LEAD

TO GET THE MOST FROM THIS STUDY, READ THE PREFACE AND pages 114–121 of *The Journey.*

- Read the sidebar on pages 5–7 of the Study Guide, and be prepared to discuss the information in reference to the lesson.
- Read and respond to the entire lesson in the Study Guide. Make note of significant things the Lord teaches you as you study.
- Pray, asking God to reveal to you the truths related to this lesson that are applicable to the class members who will attend the small-group session.

LEADING THE SMALL GROUP

Introduction: Introduce the lesson by highlighting *Think About It* on pages 3–4 in the Study Guide. Write on the board the quote at the beginning of the lesson and the Scripture verse on pages 3–4.

Rewind: Call for class members to identify three situations in which they are most likely to pray. List responses on the board. Direct them to the activity in the Study Guide in which they are asked to identify the nature of their prayers. Call for volunteers to share their responses. Write on the board: **Prayer is . . .** Then call for volunteers to suggest completions to the statement. Then ask class members to identify the social structure that is responsible for spending time in prayer. Is it the government, the school system, the church, or the family? The sidebar is a more detailed description of prayer. Consider using it as additional information for this lesson.

Rethink: Direct attention to the activity in the Study Guide in which they are asked to identify the amount of time they spend each day in communication with each person listed. Point out that we often spend much more time communicating with people about things that don't matter than we do communicating with God about things that do matter. Call for class members to discuss reasons we make communicating with others so much more important than communicating with God. Ask: *If your prayer life reveals the strength of your relationship with God, how strong is that relationship?* Direct participants to use the activity in the Study Guide to record their responses.

Reflect: Call for volunteers to read the following Scriptures and to identify the settings in which Jesus prayed: Mark 1:35; Luke 22:44; and Luke 23:46. List the settings for the prayers on the board then ask class members to identify similar situations they have faced. Point out that Jesus' dependence on prayer should help us see just how important prayer is for our lives. Direct class members to use the activity in the Study Guide to list the burdens they are carrying. Call for a volunteer to read aloud Psalm 55:22. Discuss the relevance of this verse to the topic of prayer. Read aloud Philippians 4:6–7, and call for a volunteer to identify the end result of giving our burdens to Jesus Christ.

There are no required prayers that we must use; there is, however, an example of the way in which we should pray. Prayer is not a quick trip through the drive-through window in which we shout our orders to God, then circle the building to pick up what we requested. Prayer is meaningful communication with our loving Father. Authentic prayer involves two ingredients.

1. **Praise and thanksgiving is the first element of effective prayer.** Praise is our natural response to who God is. Direct class members to use the activity in the Study Guide to record in their own words who they believe God is. Continue the discussion by encouraging class members to use the activity in the Study Guide to identify the specific role God plays in their lives. Read aloud Matthew 6:9 and Ephesians 1:3. Call for volunteers to identify how Jesus and Paul viewed God.

Write **Thanksgiving** on the board and instruct class members to use the Study Guide to identify what first comes to mind when they hear the term. Call for a volunteer to read aloud Psalm 100:4. Review the verse, pointing out the manner in which we are to come to God. Call for volunteers to list some of the things for which they are thankful. List responses on the board. Read aloud James 1:17, highlighting the reason we are to be thankful to God. Read aloud 1 Thessalonians 5:18, and discuss the appropriate response to situations that don't go as we hoped they would. Being thankful to God is a way of life, not a day of the year.

2. **Confession is the second element of effective prayer.** Confession is simply agreeing with God about what you thought or did. Read aloud Acts 10:43, and identify what happens when we ask Jesus Christ into our hearts. Direct class members to use the Study Guide to identify those things that prevent them from confessing their sins. Discuss how each item listed affects our spiritual lives. Call for a volunteer to read aloud 1 John 1:9. Reaffirm the promise that God will forgive confessed sins. Call for a volunteer to read aloud Psalm 51:10. Encourage class members to make this psalm a part of their prayer lives.

React: The conclusion for this lesson is different—it is an opportunity to spend a considerable amount of time in prayer. Call for a volunteer to begin the time, then, after several moments, close the time of prayer. Be sure to include in your prayer the elements of effective prayer discussed in this lesson.

LEARNING TO PRAY

CHAPTER TWO

THE PROCESS OF PRAYER

PREPARE TO LEAD

TO GET THE MOST FROM THIS STUDY, READ PAGES 121–123 OF *The Journey.*

- Read the sidebar on pages 23–24 of the Study Guide, and be prepared to discuss the information in reference to the lesson.
- Read and respond to the entire lesson in the Study Guide. Make note of significant things the Lord teaches you as you study.
- Pray, asking God to reveal to you the truths related to this lesson that are applicable to the class members who will attend the small-group session.

LEADING THE SMALL GROUP

Introduction: Introduce the lesson by highlighting *Think About It* on pages 21–22 in the Study Guide. Write on the board the quote at the beginning of the lesson and the Scripture verse on page 21.

Rewind: As class members arrive, instruct them to use the activity in the Study Guide to write a prayer they might pray, and then to use the activity that follows in the Study Guide to evaluate the focus of that prayer. Discuss the reality that many prayers are more focused on personal wants and needs rather than on praising God for who He is. The sidebar for this lesson focuses on models of prayer. It will be helpful to review the sidebar before leading the lesson.

Rethink: Write on the board **Broken and Contrite Heart** and call for volunteers to suggest possible meanings for the phrase. List responses on the board. Explain that prayer involves two hearts—God's and ours. Ask class members to reflect on their lives and to determine whose heart is more broken over their sin—God's or theirs. Explain that seeing life from God's perspective will change the way we view our sin. Only as we communicate with God can we really have a broken and contrite heart.

Reflect: In order for our prayers to be effective, we must evaluate our lives based on the following six guidelines.

1. **Have the right attitude.** Direct participants to use the activity in the Study Guide to evaluate the regularity with which they pray. Point out that not praying indicates that God isn't needed and that praying

regularly indicates a dependence on God. Discuss some of the reasons people don't spend time in prayer. Read aloud 1 Peter 5:5, and insert your name in place of "the proud." Encourage the class members to do the same. Discuss what this verse says about our attitudes toward God and His desire to be a part of our lives.

2. **Seek God's will in your prayers.** Direct class members to use the activity in the Study Guide to identify the elements of their most recent prayer. Point out that it is easy to give God His orders for the day, then sit back and wait for Him to work. Ask class members why this strategy won't work. Discuss responses. Point out that prayer isn't about convincing God to see things our way; it's about our being transformed so that we can see things from God's perspective. Read aloud Mark 10:38, and identify how Jesus responded to inappropriate prayers. Read James 4:3 to discover why we don't get many of the things for which we pray. Read aloud Matthew 6:10, and direct class members to use the activity in the Study Guide to identify the meaning of this verse.

3. **Bring everything to God in prayer.** Read aloud Philippians 4:6, and discuss the need to take everything to God in prayer. Discuss why people only pray during a crisis. Ask volunteers to identify themselves as crisis pray-ers or constant pray-ers.

4. **Learn to pray at all times and in all situations.** We have a misconception about prayer in that we think we have to have our eyes closed and our heads bowed. There is nothing wrong with those

actions in association with prayer, but they aren't required. Read aloud 1 Thessalonians 5:17, and highlight its significance in light of the command to pray at all times.

5. **Trust God for the outcome.** We like to fix things, and we aren't very patient. Direct class members to use the activity in the Study Guide to identify the reasons God doesn't answer our prayers the way we desire. Call for a volunteer to recall a personal story related to persistent prayer. Point out that prayer is more about changing our attitudes than changing God's mind.

6. **Learn to listen.** Read aloud Psalm 37:7. Discuss the danger of not listening to God. Describe a time when you acted without listening to God.

React: As you bring the lesson to a close, lead the class through the activities in the React section of the Study Guide. As appropriate, call for volunteers to share their thoughts related to each question.

Call attention to the "Three Truths" activity at the end of the lesson. Be prepared to share your three truths as an example. Close in prayer.

LEARNING TO PRAY

CHAPTER THREE

EMOTIONS THAT DEFEAT US

PREPARE TO LEAD

TO GET THE MOST FROM THIS STUDY, READ PAGES 175–184 OF *The Journey.*

- Read the sidebar on pages 39–40 of the Study Guide, and be prepared to discuss the information in reference to the lesson.
- Read and respond to the entire lesson in the Study Guide. Make note of significant things the Lord teaches you as you study.
- Pray, asking God to reveal to you the truths related to this lesson that are applicable to the class members who will attend the small-group session.

LEADING THE SMALL GROUP

Introduction: Introduce the lesson by highlighting *Think About It* on pages 37–38 in the Study Guide. Write on the board the quote at the beginning of the lesson and the Scripture verse on pages 37–38.

Rewind: Call for volunteers to list some of the emotions they experience on a regular basis. List responses on the board, then ask class members to identify the emotions that they experience most often. Circle their responses on the board. Direct class members to use the activity in the Study Guide to identify how their emotions affect their relationship with God and their vulnerability to the attacks of Satan. The sidebar for the lesson is on the wrath of God. If appropriate, include this material in the discussion of this lesson.

Rethink: Review the list of emotions that was written on the board in the first part of the lesson. Ask class members to identify emotions that are most effective in revealing God's character to people who do not know Him. Direct class members to use the activity in the Study Guide to identify emotions that are part of their natural responses to people. Discuss how effective their emotions are in revealing God's true character. Point out that emotions can be used to praise God or to ruin relationships. The trick for believers is to control the damaging emotions while exhibiting emotions that point people to God.

Reflect: In this lesson, we will focus on two pairs of emotions that can be devastating in the lives of believers—anger and bitterness, along with worry and fear.

1. **Anger and bitterness.** Direct the class members to use the activity in the Study Guide to identify the situations that they have faced. Call

for volunteers to share stories about the role of anger in the situations they faced. Call for a volunteer to read aloud Mark 14:71 and to identify the situation in which this verse took place. Then call for a volunteer to read aloud Ephesians 4:13 and to identify Paul's advice for the Christians in Ephesus. Anger isn't always directed at other people; it can be directed at God. Call for volunteers to identify some situations in which someone might become angry at God. Some anger is justified. Read aloud Matthew 21:12–13, and discuss the situation in which Jesus became angry. Point out that Jesus' anger was related to the damage that was being done to God's reputation. Ask: *Are you more likely to become angry about your reputation being damaged or God's reputation being damaged? Why?* Discuss responses.

Anger and bitterness often travel together. People who remain angry over a long period of time become bitter. Read aloud Hebrews 12:15, and discuss situations that cause believers to grow bitter. Brainstorm some things that can be done to prevent bitterness from taking over a person's life. Read aloud Ephesians 4:22–24, and discuss the changes that are required if someone is going to overcome bitterness in his or her life. Read aloud Matthew 5:22; Proverbs 29:22; and Psalm 37:8, and encourage class members to use the activity in the Study Guide to explain the ultimate danger of remaining angry and bitter.

Anger and bitterness reflect an attitude toward other people that is inconsistent with God's will. Read aloud Luke 6:28 and Ephesians 4:32 to locate the attitudes we are to have toward all people—even those with whom we are most likely to become angry.

2. **Worry and fear.** Fear can be used to protect us, but it also can paralyze us. Read aloud Proverbs 22:3, then suggest that class members use the space provided in the Study Guide to write personal paraphrases of the verse. There is plenty of biblical advice regarding fear. Read aloud 1 Peter 5:8, and discuss the concepts of being self-controlled and alert.

Worry is simply an inordinate amount of time spent thinking about situations that cannot be changed or controlled. Call for volunteers to identify some of the things about which they worry. List responses on the board. Discuss the spiritual effect of worry and a strategy for giving our concerns to God. Read aloud Psalm 118:6, and relate it to the concept of worry.

React: The antidote to undesired emotions is faith. The more we focus on strengthening our faith, the less likely we are to worry. Review the strategy in the React section of the Study Guide before closing the session.

Call attention to the "Three Truths" activity at the end of the lesson. Be prepared to share your three truths as an example. Close in prayer.

LEARNING TO PRAY

CHAPTER FOUR

THINGS THAT DESTROY

PREPARE TO LEAD

TO GET THE MOST FROM THIS STUDY, READ PAGES 185–194 OF *The Journey.*

- Read the sidebar on pages 59–60 of the Study Guide, and be prepared to discuss the information in reference to the lesson.
- Read and respond to the entire lesson in the Study Guide. Make note of significant things the Lord teaches you as you study.
- Pray, asking God to reveal to you the truths related to this lesson that are applicable to the class members who will attend the small-group session.

LEADING THE SMALL GROUP

Introduction: Introduce the lesson by highlighting *Think About It* on pages 57–58 in the Study Guide. Write on the board the quote at the beginning of the lesson and the Scripture verse on page 57.

Rewind: As class members arrive, instruct them to work together in pairs or in small groups to respond to the first activity in the Rewind section of the Study Guide. Before continuing, allow class members to spend some time quietly reflecting on their lifestyles and considering their personal integrity. Read aloud 1 Corinthians 10:12, and discuss Paul's warning to the Christians in Corinth. The sidebar focuses on the concept of being self-controlled. Before continuing the lesson, take the time to review the information in the sidebar and consider ways that it might be helpful in leading this lesson.

Rethink: Call for volunteers to report some of the warnings they were given as children. List responses on the board. After a few moments, discuss the potential consequences of ignoring the warnings. List some of the consequences on the board. Recount stories about frivolous litigation and how people today often avoid responsibility for their actions. Remind the class, however, that we all one day will be forced to account for what we have done. To avoid bad consequences, we must make better decisions.

Reflect: In an earlier lesson, we discussed the concept of being principled people rather than rule-following people. Ask class members to identify the differences between the two concepts. Arrange the class in small groups, and call for them to use the Study Guide activity to identify the decision-making processes of people who live by the rules and people who live based on principles. After a few moments, call for groups to report their findings. Enlist a volunteer to read aloud John 14:15 and identify the true test of our love for God. Direct class members to use the activity in the Study Guide to mark their love for God based on their obedience to Him.

Point out that Satan knows our weaknesses and has a strategy to attack us at our weakest points. Review the activity in the Study Guide, and identify Satan's goal for each person. If we are going to defend ourselves against Satan's attacks, we must focus on developing four character qualities.

1. **Integrity.** Write **Integrity** on the board, and call for volunteers to suggest meanings. List responses on the board. Ask: *Would you want your private life revealed to the general public?* Explain that our answers to that question reveal our personal integrity. Read aloud 1 Chronicles 29:17, and identify what pleases God. Write the response on the board. Allow a few moments for class members to use the Study Guide to evaluate the integrity they demonstrate in the listed areas of their lives. If we are consistent in our lifestyles (as compared to God's standard), then God is winning the battle in our lives. However, if we find ourselves lacking integrity in any area, it is because we have given control of that area to Satan.

2. **Honesty.** Write **Honesty** on the board, and call for volunteers to suggest meanings. List responses on the board. Read aloud Leviticus 19:11, and discuss the lesson contained in this verse. Call for volunteers to recount situations in which they have dealt with honest or dishonest

people. Ask: *In what areas of life are we most likely to be dishonest?* List responses on the board. Read aloud John 8:44, and describe Satan's role in the world. Call for volunteers to share some forms of dishonesty in which Christians often engage. Be sure to include gossip on the list. Point out that sharing damaging personal information "as a matter of prayer" still is gossiping. If we are praying to God, He knows the situation; if we are talking about other people, it's gossip. Read aloud Proverbs 20:19 and 2 Corinthians 12:20, pointing out what each verse says about gossip.

3. **Purity.** Write **Purity** on the board and call for definitions. List responses on the board. Define purity as "the absence of immorality and perversion." Call for a volunteer to read aloud Jeremiah 6:15, then discuss the relevance of the verse to today's culture. One area with which we struggle is sexual immorality—both in thought and in action. Call for volunteers to identify some sources of sexual immorality. List responses on the board. Call for a volunteer to read aloud 1 Corinthians 6:18. If the things listed on the board represent sexual immorality, based on 1 Corinthians 6:18, what should be a Christian's response? Discuss how Christians can flee music, television, movies, and so forth. Point out that anything sexual outside the bounds of marriage is sexual perversion and is immoral.

4. **Freedom.** Write **Freedom** on the board, and call for volunteers to describe Christian freedom. List responses on the board. Explain that Christian freedom is freedom from sin's control, freedom from guilt, freedom from sin's consequences, and freedom from sin's power. Read

aloud John 8:34–36, and discuss the source of a believer's freedom. Satan wants us to remain in bondage to sin and its power; Jesus wants us to be free from sin's power. One of these forces is winning in each of our lives.

React: To close this lesson, work systematically through the React section of the Study Guide. Be sure to read aloud the Scriptures that are listed.

Call attention to the "Three Truths" activity at the end of the lesson. Be prepared to share your three truths as an example. Close in prayer.

LEARNING TO PRAY

CHAPTER FIVE

WHEN LIFE TURNS AGAINST US

PREPARE TO LEAD

TO GET THE MOST FROM THIS STUDY, READ PAGES 195–204 OF *The Journey.*

- Read the sidebar on pages 79–81 of the Study Guide, and be prepared to discuss the information in reference to the lesson.

- Read and respond to the entire lesson in the Study Guide. Make note of significant things the Lord teaches you as you study.

- Pray, asking God to reveal to you the truths related to this lesson that are applicable to the class members who will attend the small group session.

LEADING THE SMALL GROUP

Introduction: Introduce the lesson by highlighting *Think About It* on pages 77–78 in the Study Guide. Write on the board the quote at the beginning of the lesson and the Scripture verse on pages 77–78.

Rewind: Write **Why?** on the board, and call for volunteers to describe the last situation they faced that caused them to ask God this question. After a few moments, call for volunteers to describe how their situations affected their faith relationship with God. Point out that part of living in a fallen world is the reality of evil. Some people seem to have more than their fair share of negative situations, while others seemingly go unaffected. The sidebar deals with evil and why God allows it to happen. Review this material before leading the lesson.

Rethink: Direct class members to use the activity in the Study Guide to describe the worst possible thing that could happen to them and how they might respond to God if it really happened. Call for volunteers to share their responses. Read aloud Matthew 26:39, pointing out that Jesus wanted to bypass the suffering He was about to face. Yet, because He was obedient to God and He loves us, He went through with the "worst possible" situation. Jesus was perfect and didn't deserve what He got; why should we expect to avoid evil in our lives?

Reflect: Read aloud Ecclesiastes 12:1, and identify the advice it contains. Call for volunteers to identify their faith response to potential problems (using the options in the Study Guide activity). Ask a volunteer to describe a time when he or she experienced disappointment. Ask if others in the class also have experienced disappointment. It is obvious that we all experience disappointment of some kind. In response to disappointment, we experience a variety of emotions. Call attention to the list of possible responses to disappointment, and encourage class members to mark the responses that they most often have. Read aloud Isaiah 49:23, and discuss the connection between disappointment and faith. Whenever we experience disappointment and failure, we must keep three things in mind.

1. **Remember that God's love for you has not changed.** Satan wants us to believe that God stops loving us when we fail or disappoint Him. He also wants us to take our eyes off of God when we experience disappointment. Call for volunteers to identify some things that can be done to remind us of God's love. List responses on the board. Read aloud Lamentations 3:22–23, and allow time for class members to use the space provided in the Study Guide to respond to the message of this passage.

2. **Learn to keep your disappointments and failures in perspective.** Because we can't control other people and situations, we are sure to experience disappointment. When we do, we must stay focused on our relationships with God. Call attention to the activity in the Study Guide, and instruct class members to rate the significance of their most recent disappointment. Many times, a situation that seems critical at the moment is really not that significant in the grand scheme of things. When we reflect on our disappointments, we often discover that our unrealistic expectations played a role in the situations we faced. Instruct class members to use the space provided in the Study Guide to identify their roles in their most recent disappointments

and any changes they would make in their responses and/or behaviors.

3. **Learn from your disappointments and failures, and—with God's help—seek to overcome them.** Considering the fact that we all are flawed, our only hope is to trust God to see His Son rather than us. Read aloud Proverbs 12:15, and discuss the practical warning of this verse. Write **Contentment** on the board, and call for volunteers to identify those situations and/or things that represent contentment to them. List responses on the board. Read aloud Philippians 4:11, asking if this verse is true of people in the room. Point out that contentment is a spiritual condition, not a socioeconomic condition.

React: To close this lesson, work systematically through the React section of the Study Guide. Be sure to read aloud the Scriptures that are listed.

Call attention to the "Three Truths" activity at the end of the lesson. Be prepared to share your three truths as an example. Close in prayer.

LEARNING TO PRAY

CHAPTER SIX

WHEN OTHERS DISAPPOINT

PREPARE TO LEAD

TO GET THE MOST FROM THIS STUDY, READ PAGES 205–214 OF *The Journey.*

- Read the sidebar on pages 97–98 of the Study Guide, and be prepared to discuss the information in reference to the lesson.
- Read and respond to the entire lesson in the Study Guide. Make note of significant things the Lord teaches you as you study.
- Pray, asking God to reveal to you the truths related to this lesson that are applicable to the class members who will attend the small-group session.

LEADING THE SMALL GROUP

Introduction: Introduce the lesson by highlighting *Think About It* on pages 95–96 in the Study Guide. Write on the board the quote at the beginning of the lesson and the Scripture verse on pages 95–96.

Rewind: As class members arrive for the session, instruct them to use the activity in the Study Guide to identify their three most significant relationships and the disappointment that is associated with each relationship. Call for volunteers to identify how they normally respond to disappointment. List responses on the board. Any time there are two people, we have the potential of being disappointed. Because we are selfish people, we often experience disappointment simply because people don't do what we want them to do. The sidebar for this lesson is on the concept of coveting and should be included as part of this study.

Rethink: Call for volunteers to identify the cause of their most recent conflict with another person. List brief summaries of each response on the board. Read aloud Matthew 15:19, and identify the attitudes and actions Jesus addressed. Rhetorically ask: *Which of these attitudes or actions is a problem for you?* Our actions toward other people serve to reveal God to them. The issue is the accuracy of our revelation of God. Ask: *When people see you respond to what others do, is your response consistent with God's character?* Call for volunteers to identify why it is so hard to respond to disappointment with godliness.

Reflect: Call for a volunteer to read aloud Micah 6:8 and identify the three things that should be the priorities for God's people. Encourage class members to write their responses in the space provided in the Study Guide. Point out that there are two relationships highlighted in Micah 6:8—the relationship with God and the relationship with other people. Selfishness is rooted in misplaced love; rather than loving God or others, we love ourselves. This is not just a problem for other people; it is a problem for us. Call for a volunteer to read aloud 1 Peter 4:8 and Ephesians 4:22–23, then discuss the principles contained in these passages. Discuss what happens when we begin to see other people the way God sees them. List responses on the board. Call for a volunteer to read aloud Philippians 2:4, then discuss some ways this verse can become a reality in our everyday lives.

Scripture offers seven principles that should govern our relationships with other people. As you work through each principle listed, read aloud the Scripture and discuss it in its context.

1. **Mark 9:50.** Jesus instructed His followers to make living at peace with others a priority. That means diffusing situations before they escalate into problems. The same challenge is extended in Hebrews 12:14.

2. **Matthew 7:12.** This has been referred to as the Golden Rule. We have seen variations of the rule and sometimes are confused as to what it really says. Jesus said to treat others the way we want to be treated. If you treat other people rudely, you should expect the same. So many times we are most aggravated at the actions of other people that are the very things we do in the same situations.

3. **Matthew 5:43–44.** We should pray for everyone—those we consider friends and those we consider enemies. If God never dismisses

anyone from His concern, we don't have the option of dismissing people either.

4. **Psalm 141:3.** Once spoken, words cannot be retracted. The damage is done and the cleanup begins. That's why Scripture warns us to guard our words. This means measuring our words carefully and making sure that our words don't contradict the character of the God we claim to serve. Read aloud James 3:6, and call for volunteers to describe times when their words led to an interpersonal conflict. Discuss the steps that could have been taken to avoid the conflict.

5. **Romans 12:17, 19.** When we are the victims of something someone did, we often seek revenge against that person. But rather than serving to defuse the situation, revenge escalates it. Eventually, the relationship is permanently damaged and God's reputation harmed. We can't allow hate to control us.

6. **John 8:36.** Sometimes we can't escape the past. Maybe we did something that is a source of embarrassment or leads us to consider ourselves as failures. We can't hold onto the past. If God forgives us, we should forgive ourselves and move on.

7. **Colossians 3:13.** We are quick to accept forgiveness but slow to grant it. However, our failure to grant forgiveness makes us slaves to the events of the past. We can't move forward while looking behind us.

React: To close this lesson, work systematically through the React section of the Study Guide. Be sure to read aloud the Scriptures that are listed.

Call attention to the "Three Truths" activity at the end of the lesson. Be prepared to share your three truths as an example. Close in prayer.

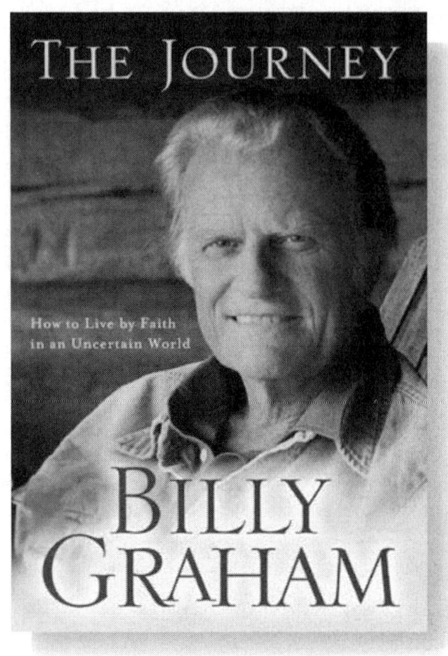

Billy Graham is respected and loved around the world. *The Journey* is his magnum opus, the culmination of a lifetime of experience and ministry. With insight that comes only from a life spent with God, this book is filled with wisdom, encouragement, hope, and inspiration for anyone who wants to live a happier, more fulfilling life.

978-0-8499-1887-2 (PB)